THE ECOLOGICAL
PERSPECTIVE

PUBLISHED FOR THE

PRINCETON CENTER OF

INTERNATIONAL STUDIES

BY PRINCETON UNIVERSITY PRESS

PRINCETON, NEW JERSEY 1965

A LIST OF OTHER CENTER PUBLICATIONS

APPEARS AT THE BACK OF THE BOOK

THE ECOLOGICAL

PERSPECTIVE ON

HUMAN AFFAIRS

WITH SPECIAL

REFERENCE TO

INTERNATIONAL

POLITICS

BY HAROLD AND

MARGARET SPROUT

FOREWORD

In 1956 the Center of International Studies circulated informally an essay by Professor and Mrs. Sprout, entitled "Man-Milieu Relationship Hypotheses in the Context of International Politics." That essay was sent to several hundred geographers, political scientists, and other social scientists in America and abroad. With each copy the Center enclosed a card inviting criticism or other comment. The response was much greater than expected.

The "Man-Milieu" essay has been out of print since the summer of 1957, but requests for copies still come in frequently. This evidence of continuing interest and the wide range of reactions from readers have encouraged the authors to re-examine the issues discussed in the earlier essay. The result is the present work, in which they have modified and enlarged the frame of inquiry.

More specifically, the authors examine critically and comparatively several philosophical postures toward, and modes of dealing with, the relations of individuals, variously constituted groups, political communities as a whole, and other complex organizations to the conditions, human as well as nonhuman, that are said to environ them. Special consideration is given to the uses of environmental concepts and theories in the analysis of foreign policies, in the estimation of the international capabilities of states, in the interpretation of international history, and in the description and explanation of the patterns of interaction that comprise in the aggregate what is called the international system.

The earlier "Man-Milieu" essay was sometimes discussed as if it represented a new theoretical approach to the study of politics. Nothing so pretentious was contemplated then—or now. The present work represents simply an attempt to clarify and straighten out certain semantic and conceptual issues that are implicit in any theory of politics, or, indeed, in any discussion of human endeavor and achievement in any field. In this connection, readers will note the authors' rather provocative conclusions regarding usage of environmental terms and relational ideas with reference to abstract entities such as the state, the political system, and the international system.

The authors have chosen to focus their examination of environmental concepts and theories on international politics for two reasons: first, because of their long association with this field of study; second, because the high level of abstraction at which much of the discussion of diplomacy, war, and other international phenomena is pitched, puts into sharp relief some of the more troublesome issues posed by generally prevailing usage of environmental terms, concepts, and theories. For this reason, among others, the work may well serve as prolegomena—in my opinion, essential prolegomena—to the study of foreign policy and international politics.

However, much of what is said in this book is just as relevant to contexts other than political. Readers will note, in this connection, that many of the illustrative examples are drawn from nonpolitical fields. They will note too that the environmental concepts and relationship theories examined in the following chapters come mainly from outside the discipline of politics—in particular, from the disciplines of geography and psychology, and from the philosophies of science and history. The work thus emphasizes the pervasiveness of the "ecological perspective" and of environmental concepts and theories in all approaches to the study of human affairs.

Mr. and Mrs. Sprout are co-authors of works on the

FOREWORD

political history of the American Navy, and of more general works in international politics. Since 1952, Mr. Sprout
has occupied the Henry Grier Bryant Professorship of
Geography and International Relations in Princeton University. He is also a faculty associate of the Center of
International Studies.

KLAUS KNORR

Princeton, N.J.
January 1, 1965.

AUTHORS' ACKNOWLEDGMENTS

As PROFESSOR KNORR has indicated in his Foreword, this work represents a further development of themes discussed in our earlier essay, *Man-Milieu Relationship Hypotheses in the Context of International Politics*. That essay was one of the products of a grant by the Rockefeller Foundation to Princeton University, to promote studies designed to bring the disciplines of geography and politics into more productive relationships. Thus the first acknowledgment goes appropriately to those officers of the Foundation and to the central Administration of Princeton University, without whose support it is unlikely that either the earlier essay or the present work would ever have been undertaken.

We also owe a great deal to the Center of International Studies. The Center has provided necessary financial support. An early draft of the present work was discussed in the Center's research seminar. Later drafts have been read in whole or in part by Professor Carl G. Hempel of the Princeton Department of Philosophy, and by Professor Richard Hartshorne of the Department of Geography of the University of Wisconsin. From these and other scholars we have received many helpful criticisms and suggestions, and we are grateful for them. But we alone, of course, are responsible for the work in its final form.

Finally, our indebtedness extends to a much wider community of scholars. As Professor Knorr has stated in the Foreword, our earlier essay on *Man-Milieu Relationship Hypotheses* evoked reactions from many quarters. In published reviews, in personal correspondence, and in conversations, we received criticisms and suggestions from scores

AUTHORS' ACKNOWLEDGMENTS

of scholars in America and abroad—from geographers, psychologists, sociologists, economists, historians, and philosophers of science and history, as well as from fellow political scientists. We have mentioned specifically, at appropriate places in the footnotes, some who were exceptionally generous with their time, and whose reactions to the *Man-Milieu* essay have proved to be especially productive and helpful in preparing the present work.

CONTENTS

1

THE ECOLOGICAL PERSPECTIVE

THE UNITED STATES government spends hundreds of millions of dollars annually to compile, classify, interpret, and store huge quantities of information about foreign lands and peoples. These activities occupy thousands of officials in government agencies, and experts of many kinds in private research organizations, business corporations, and universities. Comparable activities, though generally on a rather smaller scale, are carried on in other countries and (with somewhat different purposes in view) in the United Nations and other international organizations.

All this accumulation and analysis of "intelligence" has come to be regarded as an essential function of government, necessary to effective conduct of diplomacy, transnational public relations, subversion and internal war, economic and technical assistance to modernizing societies, support of allies and weakening of potential enemies, as well as necessary to the preparation of a sound military defense. Successful international statecraft, in short, is held to require a very wide range of precise and up-to-date information regarding the earth's surface, subsurface, atmosphere, and outer space, and regarding the organized political communities that comprise what is loosely called the society of nations.

This posture, it is true, is of quite recent origin. Before World War II, for example, the United States had no Central Intelligence Agency. The intelligence-gathering divisions of the War and Navy Departments were operated chiefly by men of narrow professional outlook and limited knowledge of international politics. Research and analysis

· 1 ·

in the Department of State were similarly restricted, with most professional diplomats profoundly skeptical of research and analysis not immediately connected with current problems.

However, long before the recent mushroom growth of intelligence gathering and analysis, the vocabulary of diplomacy and the rhetoric of international statecraft included many recurring words and sentences that attested to the awareness of statesmen to the relevance of environing conditions and events. Washington, in his Farewell Address, spoke of Europe's "set of primary interests, which to us have none, or a very remote relation." Jefferson emphasized the "wide ocean" that "separated" the United States from Europe. Monroe contended that "our peace and happiness" would be endangered if the Great Powers of Europe should "extend their political system" to any part of the Americas.

In 1907, a British diplomat, Sir Eyre Crowe, asserted that "the general character of England's foreign policy is determined by the immutable conditions of her geographical situation. . . ." In the same year, another British statesman, Sir Edward Frey, spoke of "the duty of every country to protect itself against its enemies and against the dangers by which it may be threatened. . . ."

In 1911, the rising British politician David Lloyd George asserted that "the peace of the world is much more likely to be secured if all nations realize fairly what the conditions of peace must be. . . ." A generation later, another British statesman, Stanley Baldwin, told the House of Commons: Since the advent of airpower, "the old frontiers are gone. When you think of the defense of England you no longer think of the chalk cliffs of Dover; you think of the Rhine. That is where our frontier lies."

When Russian-supported activities, following World War II, were believed in Washington to be designed to convert Greece into a Soviet satellite, President Truman informed Congress that "totalitarian regimes imposed on free peoples, by direct or indirect aggression, undermine the foundations of international peace and hence the security of the United States."

A few years later a commission, appointed by the President to look into the situation of the United States with regard to raw materials, based its recommendations on the premise that "materials strength is a prime ingredient of rising living standards in peace and of military strength in war."

Such statements are common currency of international statecraft. All exemplify the truism that those who conduct foreign relations and formulate defense policies are keenly aware, as a rule, of the relevance of surrounding conditions and events, and of the disasters that may overwhelm them through failure to take such factors into account. Sometimes the environmental basis of a decision or of a political relationship is formulated explicitly. More often it is simply implicit in the words and phrases employed. In either case, the point of interest here is that statesmen, like everyone else, justify their decisions and explain their successes and failures by reference to surrounding conditions and events.

This mode of thinking and speaking also pervades unofficial commentaries on international politics. Captain Alfred Thayer Mahan concluded, about 1900, that two sets of obstacles stood in the way of Russian expansion into the Far East and Indian Ocean areas: obstacles implicit in Russian geography, and obstacles imposed by the strategies and capabilities of the great maritime Powers.

In 1919, the British geographer Sir Halford Mackinder began a memorandum to the diplomats assembling for the Peace Conference in Paris, with the thesis that "the great wars of history . . . are the outcome, direct or indirect, of the unequal growth of nations, and that unequal growth is not wholly due to the greater genius and energy of some nations as compared with others; in large measure it is the result of the uneven distribution of fertility and strategical opportunty upon the face of the globe." [1]

In the early 1930's, Brooks Emeny stated a thesis that has become a truism in our time. He said: ". . . capacity for industrialization [is the key to a state's future power position]. And since large-scale industrialization presupposes the possession or ready availability of vast quantities of the basic industrial materials, Nature, through her unequal distribution of these, has rigidly set a limit to the number of states capable of achieving the status of Great Powers." [2]

Against the historic maxim that "God is always on the side of the biggest battalions," the demographer Frank W. Notestein has contended that "the huge population of Asia . . . and its very high birth rates are not the threat to our leadership that they may seem. . . . For some decades to come the situation in Asia spells poverty and not power. . . ." [3]

More recently, the British scientist B. K. Blount has propounded a hypothesis regarding future trends in international politics, derived from well-established demographic trends, from the recognized political significance of technology, and from the assumption that the incidence of scientific geniuses and other exceptionally gifted individuals varies in proportion to the population of nations. From these ingredients, Blount derives the hypothesis that "in the future (though the transition may take a little time)

[1] H. J. Mackinder, *Democratic Ideals and Reality*, Holt, 1919, reprinted 1942, pp. 1-2.
[2] Brooks Emeny, *The Strategy of Raw Materials*, Macmillan, 1934, p. 1.
[3] F. W. Notestein, "Population," in *Scientific American*, September 1951.

power will move away from the relatively small, now highly advanced nations, and the great centers of population in Asia will come into their own. China and India will become the leading nations, eclipsing, perhaps, even Russia and the United States, and the little countries of Europe —Britain and Germany, France and Holland—will sink into obscurity." [4]

The point at issue here is not whether Blount's hypothesis, and the others previously quoted, have been or presumably will be confirmed by events. We cite them simply as further exhibits of the nearly universal practice of explaining past events and predicting future trends in the patterns of international politics by reference to some set of environmental factors.

The same practice is observed in the teaching of international politics. Nearly all contemporary textbooks give attention to the "factors" that "influence" or "condition" the "policies" and "affect" the "capabilities" and "relations" of interacting nations. These "foundations" or "elements" of national power are expounded under such rubrics as "geography," "natural resources," "industrial capacity," "population," "national character," "national morale," "military preparedness," and "quality of diplomacy" and of "government." [5]

Theorists of international politics frequently deploy environmental terms and ideas. "Setting" is one of the central concepts in the scheme for analysis of foreign-policy decision-making formulated by R. C. Snyder and his associates: a concept defined as "categories of potentially rele-

<hr/>

[4] B. K. Blount, "Science Will Change the Balance of Power," in *The New Scientist*, June 27, 1957.

[5] These rubrics are used by H. J. Morgenthau, in his widely influential text, *Politics Among Nations*, 3rd edition, Knopf, 1960. Similar headings appear in most other textbooks of international politics.

vant factors and conditions which may affect the action of any state." [6]

Various theorists have adopted or adapted David Easton's well-known concept of the "environment in which the system exists. . . ." [7] R. N. Rosecrance gives attention to phenomena that he calls the "environmental capacity" of the international system, and to "environmental constraints" on international actors.[8] J. N. Rosenau speaks of "changes that occur both within systems and within their environments. . . ." [9] C. F. Alger examines consequences of changes in the "environment" of the international system.[10]

The vocabulary of international political theory, the rhetoric of statesmen and of unofficial interpreters of international events, and the intelligence operations of governments, all attest the pervasiveness of modes of speaking that link political behavior and patterns of interaction with encompassing conditions and events, variously designated the situation, setting, stage, arena, environment, or milieu. Yet, with remarkably few exceptions, those who practice statecraft, and those who interpret and theorize about international politics from the sidelines, characteristically employ environmental terms loosely and imprecisely. They seldom exhibit much awareness of the connotations of such words and phrases. They exhibit even less concern with the instrumental mechanisms of man-environment relationships which, as a general rule, they

[6] R. C. Snyder *et al.*, *Foreign Policy Decision Making*, Free Press, 1962, p. 67.

[7] David Easton, "An Approach to the Analysis of Political Systems," in *World Politics*, 1957, v. 9, p. 384.

[8] R. N. Rosecrance, *Action and Reaction in World Politics*, Little, Brown, 1963, pp. 221, 291, 292, and *passim*.

[9] J. N. Rosenau, "The Functioning of International Systems," in *Background*, 1963, v. 7, p. 115.

[10] C. F. Alger, "Comparison of Intranational and International Politics," in *American Political Science Review*, 1963, v. 57, p. 409.

simply take uncritically for granted. Few theorists and still fewer interpreters of political events seem to be even dimly aware of the semantic and conceptual puzzles that lurk in their vocabulary and rhetoric, or of the historic controversies that have raged around different modes of connecting up environmental conditions and events with human endeavors and achievements.[11]

Viewing human individuals, groups, and organizations in their associations with one another and with nonhuman conditions and events sets a frame of reference and a mode of analysis that have come rather generally to be called "human ecology."[12] There have been attempts to identify geography with human ecology,[13] though few geographers these days would accept this identification. Human ecology is often treated as a branch of sociology. Be that as it may. We are less concerned here with disciplinary identifications than with a perspective that pervades nearly all approaches to the study of human affairs, though under variant terminologies, and oftener by implication than by specification.

The ecological perspective also pervades the subhuman branches of biology; and some of the central concepts and

[11] For a review of environmental doctrines and controversies from classical Greece to the early 1920's, see Franklin Thomas, *The Environmental Basis of Society*, Century, 1925.

[12] There is a considerable and varied literature on the ecological perspective and its human ramifications and implications. For a brief characterization, see R. D. McKenzie, "Human Ecology," in *Encyclopedia of the Social Sciences*, 1931, v. 5, pp. 314-15. For a more comprehensive and very thorough examination of the ecological perspective in social analysis, see O. D. Duncan and L. F. Schnore, "Cultural, Behavioral, and Ecological Perspectives in the Study of Social Organization," in *American Journal of Sociology*, 1959, v. 65, pp. 132*ff*.

[13] See, for example, H. H. Barrows, "Geography as Human Ecology," in *Annals*, Association of American Geographers, 1923, v. 13, pp. 1*ff*; also W. L. White and G. T. Renner, *Geography: An Introduction to Human Ecology*, Appleton-Century, 1936.

theories of human ecology are derived and adapted from observations of, and theories about, the behavior of sub-human organisms. Ideas so derived may entail odd and unanticipated consequences when applied uncritically to human activities. But even odder consequences may flow from too literal application of terms and theories, formulated with reference to flesh-and-blood human persons, to abstract entities such as the state, the political system, or the international system. This practice, long evident but apparently on the increase these days, is one of the central issues with which this essay is concerned. We shall return to it repeatedly in the chapters to come.

The ecological perspective directs attention to various kinds of phenomena. These include, among others: (1) the *psychological behavior* of persons (singly and in groups of various kinds); (2) *undertakings* or strategies designed to achieve envisaged goals or purposes; and (3) the *outcomes,* or operational results, of such undertakings, including outcomes that are unintended as well as those that are intended. With respect to all these phenomena, explanations and predictions are likely—indeed, nearly certain—to reflect some idea of environment and some hypothesis of relationship between the person or group and surrounding conditions and events.

Interest in these matters has stimulated critical re-examination of traditional modes of expressing environmental relationships. This in turn has resulted in some fresh theorizing thereon. Such theorizing is a welcome contribution to better understanding of particular human activities and achievements. It can also provide a firmer basis for generalizations regarding distributions and transformations of political and other social patterns. For these and other reasons, ecological theories may be viewed as useful tools in the workshops of social analysis.

THE ECOLOGICAL PERSPECTIVE

Critical examination of ecological concepts and theories runs into obstacles of various kinds. One is confronted by philosophical postures over which people differ profoundly and dispute interminably: for example, the ancient dispute over determinism *vs.* free will. One has also to clarify terms used differently, and often imprecisely, by geographers, psychologists, sociologists, and political analysts. Even more troublesome is the fanciful teleological rhetoric that pervades even serious works of scholarship, and the claim of those addicted to this practice that such modes of speaking affect neither what they think nor what they communicate to their fellow-men.

Especially difficult to combat is the resistance sometimes encountered to any serious examination of ecological concepts and theories at all. Some of this resistance is attributable quite clearly to scars left by the disputes over environmental determinism that raged among geographers, sociologists, philosophers, and others two or three generations ago. Alongside this residual bitterness, one also encounters widespread apathy. The nature of ecological relationships, one is told, is self-evident, and further theorizing about these is either trivial or of marginal relevance to the study of human affairs.

In our view all such arguments are mistaken. The answers to questions about environment and environmental relationships are neither self-evident nor trivial. These questions cannot "be swept under the rug" or "out the door" without taking most of the study of human affairs along, too. Even the mere use of environmental words and phrases is likely to predispose speakers toward certain modes of perceiving and interpreting events. This is so whether one is viewing the universe from the standpoint of historiography, geography, political behavior, or some other frame of reference. In short, environmental concepts and relationships are inherent in, and central to, any serious discussion of human affairs; and one's conceptions of such relationships and modes of analyzing them are certain to affect his images of the past and his expectations regarding the future. This is the thesis from which this book has taken shape.

Much of the ambiguity and confusion manifest in the use of environmental terms and in the ascription of environmental relationships can be resolved by distinguishing analytically between relations that are derived from cognition and those that are otherwise derived. This distinction involves drawing a further analytic distinction: between behavior and states of affairs resulting therefrom, or (in a more instrumental or operational sense) between what is undertaken and what is accomplished.

It may not always be possible to separate concretely these two aspects of human affairs: *undertakings* and the *outcomes thereof*. But it is analytically possible, and in our view necessary to do so in order to clear up the semantic (and inferentially, the intellectual) confusion that bedevils the use of environmental words and relational statements in the study of politics and other social phenomena. We have drawn this distinction and emphasized its importance repeatedly in the past.[14] We re-emphasize the distinction

[14] See our *Man-Milieu Relationship Hypotheses in the Context of International Politics,* Center of International Studies, Princeton University, 1956; also our "Environmental Factors in the Study of International Politics," in *Journal of Conflict Resolution,* 1957, v. 1, pp. 309*ff;* reprinted in W. A. D. Jackson *et al., Politics and Geographic Relationships,* Prentice-Hall, 1964, pp. 61*ff,* and in J. N. Rosenau *et al., International Politics and Foreign Policy,* Free Press, 1961, pp. 106*ff.* See also our "Geography and International Politics in an Era of Revolutionary Change," in *Journal of Conflict Resolution,* 1960, v. 4, pp. 145*ff;* reprinted in Jackson, *op. cit.,* pp. 34*ff;* our "Ecological and Behavioral Models in the Analysis of State Capabilities," Northwestern University, 1958 (privately circulated); and *Foundations of International Politics,* Van Nostrand, 1962, ch. 1, pp. 46*ff.*

again here at the outset, and urge that this essential point of departure be kept clearly in view throughout.[15]

In anticipation of what is to follow in later chapters, we state our main thesis as follows: So far as we can determine, environmental factors (both nonhuman and social) can affect human activities in *only two ways*. Such factors can be perceived, reacted to, and taken into account by the human individual or individuals under consideration. In this way, *and in this way only* (with one possible minor exception to be dealt with in Chapter III), environmental factors can be said to "influence," or to "condition," or otherwise to "affect" human values and preferences, moods and attitudes, choices and decisions. On the other hand, the relation of environmental factors to performance and accomplishment (that is, to the operational outcomes or results of decisions and undertakings) may present an additional dimension. In the latter context, environmental factors may be conceived as a sort of matrix, or encompassing channel, metaphorically speaking, which limits the execution of undertakings. Such limitations on performance, accomplishment, outcome, or operational result may not—often do not—derive from or depend upon the environed individual's perception or other psychological behavior. In many instances, environmental limitations on outcome or performance may be effective even though the limiting factors were not perceived and reacted to in the process of reaching a decision and initiating a course of action.

[15] Frequent failure to recognize the analytic distinction between undertakings and outcomes (in political terms, between strategies and capabilities), or, when recognized, to appreciate its importance, has been driven home to us in dozens of reactions to the earlier version of this essay, in seminar discussions of the present work, and in at least one of the reviews of *Foundations of International Politics*, 1962; see the review in *World Politics*, 1963, v. 15, pp. 342ff.

THE ECOLOGICAL PERSPECTIVE

The American debacle at Pearl Harbor is a historic example of this central thesis. The American commanders there made their defensive preparations for hostilities which they believed to be imminent. But they remained in ignorance of the approaching Japanese fleet. The environment as they perceived it contained no hostile fleet. Hence that fleet's presence was not reacted to in any way; that is to say, it had no effect whatever on the decisions of the American commanders prior to the moment of attack on that December morning in 1941. Yet the Japanese fleet was indubitably an ingredient of the environment in which the decisions of the American commanders were executed; and their ignorance of its presence did not prevent it from affecting decisively the operational outcome that occurred.

Many other examples could be cited, and some will be, in later chapters. Here it is sufficient to emphasize that this analytic distinction—between decisions and operational results, between what is undertaken and what is accomplished—is central to everything that will be said in the rest of this essay.

While our discussion of ecological perspective, concepts, and theories is set specifically in the context of international politics, much of the illustrative material (especially in the earlier chapters) is drawn from other fields, in particular from the field of human geography. This is appropriate for two reasons: (1) because geographic dimensions —identified by such terms as location, distance, space, distribution, and configuration—are nearly always significant in discussions of political undertakings and the operational results thereof; and (2) because geographers have given much attention to certain aspects of environmental relationships.

Perhaps we should insert here a few paragraphs that may seem to most geographers to be an elaboration of the obvious, but which may not be quite so obvious to many others.

THE ECOLOGICAL PERSPECTIVE

There is some tendency (probably diminishing, and discernible mainly among those relatively unfamiliar with modern geographic concepts) to think of geography as a subject that pertains chiefly to the physical earth. There can be no doubt that geographers are concerned with the physical conformation of the earth's surface: with the layout of lands and seas, the distribution of mineral rocks upon and beneath the surface, the patterns of vegetation and weather, the distribution of subhuman organisms that subsist upon the earth and on each other. All these phenomena exhibit geographic quality, in the sense that geographic science "is concerned with the arrangement of things on the face of the earth, and with the associations of things that give character to particular places." [16]

Applying this test, geographic quality also attaches to many kinds of phenomena besides the physical earth and subhuman organisms. People are geographic objects, in the sense that they are areally distributed in social groups of many kinds and sizes. The same holds for the physical structures—cultivated fields, planted forests, buildings, roads, and many other tangible structures—that human hands have superimposed upon the earth's surface, changing and often obliterating the primordial landscape. Geographic patterns are also observable in many kinds of human processes: for example, farming, manufacturing, commerce, recreation, governing; likewise, in many other intangibles of human behavior: values and norms, attitudes and preferences, customs and habits, as well as institutions and other more formal patterns. Geographic quality, in short, attaches to any phenomena—human as well as nonhuman, intangible as well as tangible—that exhibit areal dimensions and variations upon or in relation to the earth's surface.

[16] P. E. James *et al., American Geography: Inventory and Prospect*, Syracuse University Press, 1954, p. 4.

THE ECOLOGICAL PERSPECTIVE

This concept of geographic quality is central to the ecological perspective and to any scheme for analysis of ecological relationships. This is so because systematic analysis confirms the common-sense observation that the distribution and arrangement of phenomena upon the earth's surface are always, or nearly always, related significantly to what people undertake and to what they accomplish. The ecological perspective and ecological theories bring the dimensions of location, distance, space, distribution, and configuration sharply into focus in many social contexts, not least in the context of politics in general and of international politics in particular.

Every political community (though not necessarily every political organization) rests upon a geographic base. Territory is universally recognized to be one of the essential attributes of statehood. Probably the geographic exhibits most familiar to the most people are the maps that delineate the boundaries and differentiate the territories of national and subnational political communities.

The territory of each political community differs from all the rest—in location, in size and shape, in distance from the others, in arable land and climate and other so-called natural resources. Each differs from the rest in numbers of people, in their level and variety of knowledge and skills, in their mechanical equipment and stage of economic development, in their form of government, and in many other respects. All these phenomena, nonhuman and human, are unevenly distributed among the communities that comprise the society of nations. In most (if possibly not quite all) transactions among nations (and the same holds for relations among individuals and groups within national communities), at least some of the geographic dimensions noted above are certain to be significantly related to what is undertaken and also to what is accomplished.

This is conspicuously the case with transactions which exhibit some element of conflict of purpose or interest among the interacting persons, groups, or organized communities—transactions that exhibit political quality in the narrower sense of that term. Political demands and responses thereto are projected through space from one point to another upon the earth's surface. All the techniques of statecraft, domestic as well as international, involve expenditures of energy and consumption of other resources. This is obviously the case with respect to military operations and the administration of public order. But it is likewise the case in varying degrees with respect to nonsubversive public relations and propaganda, subversive conspiracy and internal war, economic and technical assistance, diplomacy and conference, and all the variants and combinations of these modes of operation. In any period of history, the results of international statecraft exhibit more or less clearly discernible patterns of coercion and submission, and influence and deference, patterns reflected in political terms with strong geographic connotations: such as balance of power, bipolarity, political orbit, satellite, bloc, coalition, alliance, the Monroe doctrine, the Atlantic community, the Near East, and many others.

The logistical aspects of statecraft have received a good deal of attention. It is generally accepted these days that the opportunities available to any state—opportunities which, in the aggregate, are sometimes called the state's power position, or its international capabilities—are related to a wide range of factors dealt with under such academic rubrics as geography, demography, economics, sociology, technology, and others. It may be less generally appreciated that *all* such phenomena, not merely those conventionally labeled geographic, exhibit areal dimensions and patterns. And there is perhaps still less appreciation of the confused state of theory regarding the political relevance of location, space, distance, distribution, and configuration, in any constellation of international political relations.

Classical political philosophers paid considerable attention to spatial distributions and dimensions. Some of them exhibited a keen sense of the relevance of the ecological viewpoint, though their conclusions generally reflected intuition rather than application of explicit ecological theories.[17] But, with certain exceptions, modern political theorists have largely ignored, or dealt only peripherally with, environmental concepts and theories. Anyone who desires to probe much below the surface in this sector of social theory will find it necessary to go to those disciplines which display more explicit interest in these matters: in particular, to geography and psychology, and, less directly but most helpfully, the philosophies of science and history.

In preparing this essay we have drawn heavily on some of this theoretical work. We have been especially interested in philosophical and methodological debates that have continued for many years within the discipline of geography. This interest derives, in considerable degree, from our long-standing conviction of the importance of geographic dimensions and distributions in explaining and predicting political behavior and relationships. But that is not the only reason. Though, as noted above, very few geographers these days would define their discipline in ecological terms, geographers nevertheless have devoted a great deal of attention to the issues involved in analyzing human relations both to the physical earth and the structures that mankind has superimposed upon the primordial landscape, and to the intangible social patterns that too exhibit areal dimensions.[18]

[17] See, for example, the summaries of classical ecological interpretations in Thomas, *The Environmental Basis of Society, passim.*
[18] We have benefited incalculably from conversations and cor-

THE ECOLOGICAL PERSPECTIVE

One not only derives benefit but also assumes certain risks when he borrows concepts and theories from cognate fields. The political analyst should always bear in mind that geographers, psychologists, logicians, philosophers of history, and other specialists working outside a specifically political frame of reference may view the universe from rather different perspectives. Conversely, geographers and psychologists, for example, should not be too surprised to discover students of politics focussing on different questions and viewing ecological relationships in ways more or less unfamiliar to them. One set of specialists may use terms unique to their own field, or conveying different meanings and nuances in other fields. Concepts transferred from one field to another may entail unanticipated consequences, not the least of which is often intellectual confusion.

One such problem will be very much with us in the chapters to come. Psychologists have built up a body of concepts and theories about human behavior, derived from observation of human subjects, supplemented by experiments with laboratory animals. So far as we can determine, these theories provide the only instrumental basis for linking the decisions of individuals (acting singly or in groups) with conditions and events that environ them. Political theorists have borrowed heavily from this stock of psychological terms and propositions; and they have applied these not only to concrete human individuals and groups but also to abstract entities such as the state, the political system, and the international system. Anticipating a conclusion to be demonstrated later, we express doubt whether this extension of psychological concepts and theories to high-level abstractions is either tenable or necessary. This is a

respondence with scores of geographers, both in Europe and in America, who read and reacted to our earlier essay, *Man-Milieu Relationship Hypotheses in the Context of International Politics.*

controversial issue, and our position thereon may not be readily acceptable to some general behavior-systems theorists. The point here is simply that theories developed with reference to one set of phenomena may or may not fit sensibly when applied to another.

We recognize that absolute precision is an unattainable will-o'-the-wisp in verbal discourse. But gross imprecision, loose usage of technical terms, and uncritical borrowing of concepts and theories from other fields can present serious, even insuperable, obstacles to any effective communication at all. Since this essay is inescapably concerned with the vocabularies and theories of several different fields, it should help to clarify what follows if we devote some space in the next chapter to delineating certain political and ecological concepts as precisely and explicitly as possible.

2

FOCAL TERMS AND CONCEPTS

PERHAPS SOME readers may feel that to take space here to examine a few key terms and concepts is to proceed rather like the lawyer who insisted on introducing evidence in court to prove what a lead-pencil is. They may even re-act like the judge, who said he would take judicial notice of the nature of lead-pencils, and instructed the lawyer to get on with his case. To anyone who queries the need for this chapter, we can only repeat that we shall be dealing with terms and concepts that appear in the technical vo-cabularies of different special fields. Such terms as politics, power, environment, and environmental relationship of-ten convey different meanings, or shades of meaning, to geographers, psychologists, political scientists, and other specialists. Such variation is also observed among differ-ent speakers in the same field, and even in the usage of a single speaker on different occasions.

Consider, to begin with, the terms *international affairs, international relations,* and *international politics.* These terms are used more or less interchangeably, often without any clearly evident referent for any of them. Sometimes the reference is to all transactions that extend into the geo-graphic space of two or more states; in other contexts, only to transactions between the governments of states. Even when restricted to intergovernmental transactions, *interna-tional politics* sometimes refers to all such transactions; in other contexts, only to those that exhibit conflict of inter-est or purpose, accompanied by some exercise of power or influence to effect an adjustment or resolution of the conflict. In general, we prefer the latter usage, but it is unnecessary to press this preference here, since ambiguity on this particular issue is not likely to prove troublesome with reference to ecological concepts and theories.[1]

Just the opposite is the case with respect to *power* and certain closely related concepts. Considerable imprecision and ambiguity surrounds the term *power* in the vocabulary of politics. The term may refer to recognized competence or legal authority to act in a specified contingency. But power may also refer to ability to get one's own way, irrespective of the allocation of authority. In the idiom of international politics, states are called Powers and are classified in hierarchies of power. Statesmen concern themselves with the balance of power. Alliances are formed to redress the balance of power, or to create a preponderance of power, or otherwise to improve the power position of the state in question. Such activities are called power politics. International politics as a whole is sometimes characterized as a struggle for power.

Such statements generally carry overtones of violence and bodily coercion, or threats thereof. In that frame of thinking, power in international politics is essentially su-

[1] We are well aware of the opposing view that our concept of international politics is too narrow: that international politics should be defined so as to include cooperative action to achieve common purposes as well as to resolve or adjust conflicts arising from antagonistic purposes. To this view we would reply simply that cooperative action, in the context of interstate relations, is often for the purpose of overcoming opposition from other sources; and that interstate relations, while not a zero-sum game as a rule, do nevertheless exhibit elements of conflict as well as mutuality. We would emphasize, furthermore, that the idea of conflict need not imply hostility in either a legal or a psychological sense. Conflicting purposes and interests, and exercise of state power and influence in connection therewith, characterize the relations of friends and allies as well as of those who regard each other as overt or potential enemies. The test of conflicting purpose also provides a useful analytic distinction between political and administrative transactions, a distinction convincingly emphasized by E. H. Carr, among others. See his *The Twenty Years' Crisis, 1919-1939*, 2nd edition, Macmillan, 1942, p. 102.

perior force, active or latent, with international political relationships determined in the long run by who coerces whom, or is presumably capable of doing so.[2]

Any such concept of power patently falls far short of covering the whole spectrum of political relationships. Many conflicts of purpose and interest—in the society of nations, as within a political community—are resolved without recourse to violence or to threatening actions. Often governments that command very inferior military forces get their way against the strongest Powers.

There have been efforts in recent years to redefine power to include behavioral effects unrelated or negligibly related to destructive, coercive, or threatening actions. Such efforts, so far as we can determine, have been largely fruitless. No matter how the word *power* is formally redefined, most people seem likely to go on talking about power as if it were largely a function of violence. One then needs a supplementary term to cover resolutions of conflicting purposes, in which violence or threats thereof are judged to be negligible or absent altogether.

The term in general use is *influence*. Whereas the obverse of coercion is submission, the obverse of influence is deference. Deferential behavior may be compliance to specific demands. But influence-deference may also cover relationships in which there are no specific demands, and those too in which conflict of purpose or interest is minimal. In such situations, one may speak of deference as recognition of prestige—that is, a reaction of respect or admiration for superior status or for noteworthy achievements in any sphere: for example, at the Olympic Games, in outer-space exploration, in the creation of works of art.

These aspects of political relationships may not be

[2] For a candid exposition of this position, see M. A. Ash, "An Analysis of Power, with Special Reference to International Politics," in *World Politics*, 1951, v. 3, pp. 218*ff*.

FOCAL TERMS AND CONCEPTS

sharply differentiated in actual cases. Usually they are not.
Hence there is need for a comprehensive term to denote
the whole spectrum of relationships, from coerced submission to specific demands, at one pole, to gratuitous
deference in the absence of specific demands, at the other.
For this purpose we have previously introduced the term
political potential, defining it as the total, or aggregative,
attraction, pull, pressure, or simply effect that one political
unit (a sovereign political community, in the context of
international politics) exerts on others.[8]

Many familiar terms of international politics denote patterns of political potential: for example, the Communist
bloc, the anti-Communist coalition, the Atlantic community, and the Monroe doctrine. The ingredients of such patterns range, we repeat, from coerced submission to gratuitous deference. Whatever the proportions of the various
ingedients, the results can be described as changes produced by the interacting units in their respective environments, which we shall define explicitly, in a moment, to
include human as well as nonhuman factors. The larger
the element of coercion, the smaller will be the psychological component of the response, as a rule; and vice versa.

In such a context, the task of the analyst is to identify
and assess the functions of those factors of the interacting
units and of their respective environments that set limits
to the operational results of their undertakings (strategies,
policies). The forms of this essentially ecological mode of
*analysis will be considered more specifically in Chapters
V, VIII, and IX.* At this point it is sufficient to state that
such an analysis yields an estimate (that is, a judgment,
whether explanatory or predictive) regarding the relative
capabilities of the interacting units.

Another term with strong ecological as well as political

[8] For further discussion of this concept, see our *Foundations of
International Politics,* Van Nostrand, 1962, pp. 158ff.

· 22 ·

connotations is *behavior*. This term recurs frequently in political discourse, and is apt to be confusing because behavior denotes rather different ideas in the vocabularies of physical, biological, and social sciences. All known definitions of human behavior include some idea of response to stimuli. As used here, behavior includes *all* such responses, not only those that are self-conscious, and not only those that are judged to be purposeful. So defined, behavior includes involuntary submission to bodily coercion, and responses that do not reach the threshold of self-conscious perception at all. Closely related, if not literally implicit in this concept of behavior, are various kinds of involuntary human movements, such as take place when a person is struck down by an unseen assassin, or dragged off to captivity by the police or a foreign invader.

Starting with this general concept of behavior, we define *action* as behavior that is consciously purposeful: that is, pointed or directed towards some state of affairs, consciously envisaged by the person whose activities are under observation. Thus defined, action is a subcategory of behavior.[4]

For all anyone can know, every event or state of affairs may be causally related to every other event or state of affairs. It is thus arbitrary, in a sense, to designate a specified action as the first in a sequence. But it is analytically convenient to do so, and to call this the initiatory or initial action. To this initial action, the response of another hu-

[4] Our definition should be distinguished from usage in certain fields of psychology, in which behavior refers to "any change in the life space—i.e., any change which is subject to psychological laws." Morton Deutsch, "Field Theory in Social Psychology," in *Handbook of Social Psychology*, edited by Gardner Lindzey, Addison-Wesley, 1954, v. 2, pp. 191*ff*. Our definition of behavior should also be distinguished from those that equate behavior with action. For example, R. C. Sheldon, "Some Observations on Theory in Social Science," in Talcott Parsons *et al.*, *Toward a General Theory of Action*, Harvard University Press, 1951, pp. 30-31.

man being is by definition the *reaction*. Reciprocal responses, whether in short or extended sequence, between two or among several parties, constitute *interaction*. Action and interaction may exhibit regularities, or patterns, in space and through time, both in the foreign policies of particular states and in the political relations of two or three or many states. As noted above, the vocabulary of international politics includes many terms that identify such patterns.

Decision, a term that recurs repeatedly in the following chapters, is defined as purposeful choice of ends or means, or both. Decision is thus a subcategory of action. In statecraft, decision is usually the end-product of more or less deliberative consideration. The sequence of behavioral events culminating in a decision is by definition the *process of decision-making.*

The state of affairs that exists after a course of action has run to some break-off point, selected more or less arbitrarily by the analyst, and which in his judgment would not have come into being without the antecedent decisions, is by definition the outcome, or consequence, or result of such decisions. In international politics, the result of decisions (undertakings, strategies, policies) may take the form of counteraction on the part of another state's human agents. A diplomatic proposal or demand evokes a rejoinder, a military move evokes a countermove, etc. In other cases the result of action may be compliance, or inaction, on the part of adverse parties. Or the result of action may take the form of alterations in the original actor's (or in the subsequent reactors') relations to nonhuman factors: as for example, when the manufacture of military equipment to coerce or intimidate other nations consumes coal, iron, and other nonrenewable resources, and thereby alters by so much the future opportunities latent in his environment.

Implicit in the concepts of action and reaction is the

idea of *feedback*. This concept identifies the psychological phenomena of selective perception, stimulus and response, and the strongly ecological concepts of *adaptation* and *manipulation*. Some of the troublesome issues involved in the use of ecological terms arise from theories that postulate feedback and other psychological phenomena in the operations of social structures, apart from the human individuals who compose and operate them.

Power, influence, political potential, behavior, action, feedback, reaction, decisions and the operational results of decisions, all carry connotations of relationship to environment. These connotations may be expressed in specifically ecological modes of speaking. Often, however, ecological perspective and relational ideas are simply latent or implicit. And more often than not, as noted in the preceding chapter, ecological terms and sentences are used loosely and imprecisely, and hence become a source of confusion rather than enlightenment.

The organizing concepts in any ecological statement are *environment, environed unit,* and the *interrelations of the two*. These concepts comprise the frame of ideas within which ecological theories have been invented and applied. As also noted in the previous chapter, implicit (when not explicit) in ecological parlance is the premise that locatability in space is an essential attribute of an environed unit and its environment. In the absence of this spatial dimension, ecological concepts have no more than analogical or metaphorical relevance. For this and other reasons to be elaborated later, ecological terms and modes of speaking pose refractory semantic and conceptual puzzles when used in connection with certain models and theories of international politics.

The term *environment* has a more or less standard core of meaning. Something is environed—that is, encompassed, or surrounded—and thereby related to something else in some sense that is significant. But, as previously noted, environment may mean different things in the vocabularies of geography, psychology, and other disciplines, also among different speakers within the same discipline, and even in the discourse of a single person speaking in different contexts.

Here are some of the issues in dispute. Environment may be defined as a "generic concept under which are subsumed all external forces and factors to which an organism or aggregate of organisms is actually or potentially responsive." [5] Others limit the concept to "material and spatial aspects of the surrounding world" and exclude the "web of human social relations." [6] A fairly widespread idea is that environment refers only to "natural surroundings, omitting purely man-made conditions." [7] In a well-known work on theories of social action, the general concept of environment is defined as "all those things 'outside' the organism to which action may be related." [8] Yet it is standard usage in other fields—for example, in social psychology—to include in the general concept factors that are internal as well as those that are external to the environed individual.

Sometimes one concept or another is preferred because it is assumed that the way one defines environment determines what relational theories are relevant. This is a mis-

[5] A. H. Hawley, *Human Ecology*, Ronald Press, 1950, p. 12. For a similar definition, see J. H. LeBon, *An Introduction to Human Geography*, Hutchinson, London, 1952, p. 28.

[6] J. A. Quinn, *Human Ecology*, Prentice-Hall, 1950, p. 3.

[7] R. H. Whitbeck and O. J. Thomas, *The Geographic Factor*, Appleton-Century, 1932, p. 21. The Australian geographer Griffith Taylor has objected specifically to the practice of "some geographers [who] use the term *environment* to include *every cultural factor* which affects man." *Geography in the Twentieth Century*, Philosophical Library, 1951, p. 9.

[8] Talcott Parsons, E. A. Shils, *et al., Toward a General Theory of Action*, Harvard University Press, 1951, p. 31.

taken idea. The relevance of particular theories of relationship does not depend on the kinds of factors included
in the general concept of environment. Such theories apply in exactly the same way to human and to nonhuman
factors, and to physical objects and intangible empirical
phenomena. How one conceives the environed unit may
affect the relevance of particular theories, but not what
phenomena are included in the concept of environment.

Starting from the axiom that human activities and movements may vary within limits set by human heredity and
environment, it follows that the latter, in the most comprehensive sense, includes all empirical phenomena (excepting
only the environed individual's own hereditary structures)
to which that individual may be responsive or otherwise
significantly related. Because of the tendency (noted
above) to restrict the term *environment* to nonhuman factors—and sometimes even to phenomena of nonhuman origin—we have deliberately introduced the French word
milieu. Henceforth we shall use milieu instead of environment, when the reference is general: that is, to denote the
whole spectrum of environing factors; human as well as
nonhuman, intangible as well as tangible. Unfortunately
for present purposes, the French language contains no
adjectival form of the noun *milieu,* so we shall have to make
do with the English adjective *environmental.*[9]

[9] As soon as one leaves the general concept of environment, he
encounters a veritable jungle of technical terms: for example, natural environment, nonsocial environment, physical environment,
nonhuman environment, geographic environment, social environ-
ment, ecological environment, preperceptual environment, nonpsychological environment, objective environment, subjective environ-
ment, behavioral environment, psychological environment, life
space, and still other technical terms. In some instances, the same
term stands for widely different referents in different technical
vocabularies, and sometimes even within the same vocabulary. No
one can straighten out this semantic tangle to everyone's satisfaction. For our own previous attempt to do so, see *Man-Milieu*

FOCAL TERMS AND CONCEPTS

In Chapter I we drew a distinction between the milieu as it actually is (or as it would be known to an omniscient observer, if one existed, as of course is not the case), and the milieu as it is perceived and reacted to by a particular individual. We shall henceforth call this perceived image the individual's *psycho-milieu.*

A person's psycho-milieu does not consist of phenomena external to his physical organism. His psycho-milieu consists rather of *images* or *ideas,* derived from some sort of interaction between what he selectively receives from his milieu (via his sensory apparatus) and his scheme of values, conscious memories, and subconsciously stored experience. We shall not attempt to review here the various theories regarding the nature of this psychological process. These theories lie beyond the compass of this discussion, and in any case we would not feel competent to assess them.[10] The point here is that all such theories are derived from, and purport to explain or to predict, the behavior of biological organisms. Serious difficulties arise the moment such theories are wrenched from their human-biological context and applied to abstract entities such as the state or the international system. Difficulties arise, to be more specific, because perception and cognition, stimulus and response, and other phenomena from which psychological theories are derived have no close counterparts in entities that lack the anatomical structures and physiological mechanisms and processes of biological organisms.

Relationship Hypotheses in the Context of International Politics, Center of International Studies, Princeton University, 1956, pp. 11*ff.* For some further comments on this terminological confusion, see Richard Hartshorne, *Perspective on the Nature of Geography,* Rand-McNally, 1959, pp. 55*ff.*

[10] For a summary review of these theories, see C. E. Osgood, "Behavior Theory and the Social Sciences," in Roland Young *et al., Approaches to the Study of Politics,* Northwestern University Press, 1958, pp. 217*ff.*

We shall return to this point later in the chapter and re-peatedly in the following chapters.

An individual's psycho-milieu is usually derived from phenomena which a hypothetical omniscient observer would confirm to be present in the milieu. But the refer-ent of the former term, we repeat, is the *psychological image,* not the external source from which that image is normally derived. The observer might also infer, in most instances, that image and reality are more or less congru-ent.[11] But the concept of psycho-milieu carries no built-in assumption of such congruence, and the utility of the con-cept does not depend on confirmation of congruence, points to which we shall return later (in Chapter VII) in connection with the cognitive aspect of man-milieu rela-tionships.

With one possible exception, to be considered on pages 60-63, the concept of psycho-milieu provides, so far as we can determine, the only alternative to revealed religion or mystical teleology, for relating environmental factors to an individual's moods, attitudes, choices, projects, deci-sions, and undertakings. This concept, as we have just noted, is the basis of most, if not all, modern psychological theories. Yet the distinction, between psycho-milieu (the milieu as apperceived) and the milieu as it is, is often blurred or missed altogether in political analysis.[12]

[11] Regarding the idea of reality, or the objective existence of a "real world" independent of someone's perception thereof, we do not propose to argue this ancient philosophical issue. We simply assume that there is a real world, distinct from anyone's image thereof, but knowable in practice only through the processes of perception from which are derived concepts and theories about reality.

[12] For applications of the concept of psycho-milieu in psycho-logical theory, see, for example, Morton Deutsch, "Field Theory in Social Psychology," in *Handbook of Social Psychology,* pp. 189*ff.* This concept has also been designated by various other terms, including "life space" (Kurt Lewin) and "behavioral environment,"

FOCAL TERMS AND CONCEPTS

In the execution of any decision, the complex of factors to which an individual's achievement or level of performance is significantly related is assumed to be always less than the total aggregate in his milieu. There being no omniscient observer, there are in practice no infallible criteria as to which factors are the most significant. Different observers may bring different criteria to bear. But any outside observer (that is, an observer other than the individual whose achievements are being investigated) will apply *some* criteria of relevance and significance. And by these criteria he will decide what, in his own judgment, appear to be the significant factors. The set of factors thus identified comprise (from that particular observer's perspective) the *operational milieu* of the environed individual in question. This is one of the central concepts (though not usually designated by this term) of all known systems for analyzing the military and other international capabilities of states.[18]

---

a term which we shall encounter again in Chapter VII, in William Kirk's application of the concept to historical geography.

[18] The distinctions among milieu, psycho-milieu, and operational milieu pose methodological difficulties for some social scientists. Vernon Van Dyke, in particular, objects that "phrases like . . . psychological environment . . . are a potential source of two sorts of confusion. On the one hand, they may create the impression that two different environments exist—the real one and the one that is apperceived; but obviously, an incorrect apperception of the environment is simply that, and not a different environment. On the other hand, these phrases suggest that the images one has of his environment are part of the environment; and then the distinction between the environed person and the environment is lost." *Political Science: A Philosophical Analysis*, Stanford University Press, 1960, p. 165. To Van Dyke's first objection our reply is simply that conscious behavior is demonstrably responsive to the milieu as apperceived, *and to that alone*. We do not posit two milieux, but rather one milieu which actor and observer may perceive and interpret differently. At the same time, the concept of two milieux might be a useful analytical device for emphasizing congruity or discongruity between the milieu as a specified person perceives and reacts to it, and that milieu as it appears to some outside observer who

FOCAL TERMS AND CONCEPTS

Unless one wrenches the term *environment* (and the same holds for its French equivalent *milieu*) out of etymological tradition, and gives to it a definition inconsistent with customary usage as well as technical usage in all known ecological contexts, it is imprecise if not meaningless to speak of environment without reference to some specified environed unit or class of units. There are, of course, no intrinsically "correct" definitions. One can choose to redefine old terms in new ways. For example, one might redefine environment as synonymous with the earth, or with all empirical phenomena, without connoting relationship at all. But if one intends to use the term in a relational sense (and this is clearly the sense in which it is nearly always used), then it must be recognized that there are two parts to the relation: environed unit, and the milieu to which that unit is responsive or otherwise related. We dwell on this point because of the tendency of some social scientists to use the term *environment* very loosely, often without clear reference to any environed unit at all.

If one defines milieu in a relational sense, then one has to deal with two sets of phenomena: structures and properties of the environed unit, as well as factors of the milieu. The former include those derived from heredity. Certain characters are common to the human species in general: inability to breathe under water, lack of wings to sustain flight through the air, and the like. For time-spans of in-

explains not merely decisions and undertakings but also the operational results or outcomes thereof. With respect to Van Dyke's second objection, we can only reply that the distinction between psycho-milieu and operational milieu seems to us necessary in order to identify and differentiate the kinds of man-milieu relationships implicit in the two categories of events. Until this distinction and its analytic and practical implications are more clearly understood and more consistently observed, we foresee no end to the epistemological and conceptual confusion that bedevils discussion of both the psychological and the nonpsychological aspects of man-milieu relationships.

terest to students of modern politics, human species-structures are simply treated as constant parameters, rarely even mentioned. That leaves two sets of variables: those derived from genetic variations among individuals, and those derived from the milieu.

Most students of human behavior probably agree that individual genetic variations are significant. Probably also the most credible hypothesis is that, in the long run, in large aggregates of people, the number of exceptionally gifted as well as exceptionally stupid or perverse individuals will vary in proportion to the size of the aggregate.[14] This hypothesis, however, provides no basis for predicting the incidence of specific scientific geniuses, charismatic leaders, or other exceptionally gifted individuals. One may assume that heredity has some bearing on this phenomenon; but there seems to be no agreement as to the relative importance of heredity and milieu in the making of leaders in any sphere of human activity.[15] The incidence and qualities of leaders or other gifted individuals remain for the social analyst simply variables that are likely to introduce error into any prediction of social events.

It may be practically impossible, in particular cases, to determine precisely the functions and relative importance of hereditary and environmental factors: for example, in explaining the skill of an artist or of a political leader. It may likewise be practically impossible to determine when

[14] This assumption, if tenable, could have profoundly important political implications. It is the basis of a controversial geopolitical hypothesis by the British scientist B. K. Blount. We have examined Blount's hypothesis in our "Geopolitical Hypotheses in Technological Perspective," in *World Politics*, 1963, v. 15, pp. 205ff.

[15] The biologist H. F. Blum contends that it is very difficult, if not quite impossible, to draw a precise line between human characters that are genetically derived and those that are environmentally derived but internalized in the personality of the individual. "Evolution Reconsidered," in *University, A Princeton Magazine,* Summer-Fall, 1963, pp. 3ff.

certain environing factors cease to environ. Take, for example, food upon the dining table, which is unquestionably part of the diner's milieu. At what point in the process of ingestion and digestion does the food become part of the diner and cease to be a part of his milieu? Such puzzles do not usually pose significant difficulties, any more than does the practical impossibility of disentangling environmental and hereditary contributions to the skills of the artist or the politician. In both types of cases, the problem is to identify and assess the significant limiting variables, the instrumental connections and processes involved, and the resultant state of affairs. Inability to differentiate cleanly between the structures of the environed individual and the structures of his milieu may or may not be troublesome; usually it is not, in the kinds of problems with which social scientists are concerned.

Thus far we have been speaking of human *individuals* as environed units. The concept of environed unit has been extended to human groups, to more formal organizations, and even to such abstract entities as the corporation, the state, and the political system. With reference to all of these, but especially to abstract entities, it is essential to differentiate the relations of environing factors to decisions (undertakings, strategies, policies) and to the operational results of decisions (outcomes, achievements, capabilities).

With reference to decisions, a group can be conceived in various ways. One way is to focus on the discrete individuals who, at any given moment, comprise the group. Strictly speaking, no two members of a group can envisage their respective milieux identically. This is so, among other reasons, because other members of the group comprise ingredients of the environmental image of each.[16]

---

[16] This *is* apparently what Van Dyke has in mind when he says: "Groups and political entities are not indivisible wholes surrounded externally by an environment. Rather, they are composed of indi-

FOCAL TERMS AND CONCEPTS

However, one prime attribute of a group, as generally conceived, is some degree of congruity among the members thereof, with respect to purposes, images, and modes of choosing and deciding within the range of issues with which they are collectively concerned. It is this element of congruity among members that, in most definitions, distinguishes a group from a mere congeries of individuals. This congruity enables one to speak, albeit loosely, of the group as an environed unit in the context of decisions and undertakings.

From this concept it is only a short and easy step to reification. The tendency to reify is especially evident in references to formal groups—above all, in references to the state. One cannot sense the state directly, by seeing, hearing, touching, or other sensory experience. One cannot "take a picture of a state acting." [17] Yet the literature of war and diplomacy, discussions of national character, and other political discourse are written largely in a vocabulary and style of state personification and reification.

This idiom has been carried to great lengths in some of the theorizing about political systems. Consider, for example, the following excerpts culled from an exhibit of "content analysis" applied to the "behavior of states in the international system."

"A *state* tends to operate . . . to maximize *its perceived* rewards. . . ." Certain experiences are said to be a "powerful motivating force in *both* the *individual* and the *state*. . . ." The *"system* may *elect* to accept high . . . punishment . . . either because *it perceives* . . . ," etc. "It is widely assumed that the ultimate *conscious purpose*

---

viduals, and group action is really the action of some or all of the individual members. Thus it is their individual environments that ordinarily count, and their individual environments include features that are internal to the group." *Political Science: A Philosophical Analysis,* Stanford University Press, 1960, pp. 165*f.*

[17] *Ibid.,* p. 63.

of the *state* is . . . ," etc. "A *state* may *feel* that *its status* . . . ," etc. (italics added).[18]

This is not an eccentric example. Such rhetoric is common in theoretical writings on politics, especially on international politics. Let us look at another example, in which the author categorizes the behavior of states under such psychological rubrics as "catharsis" and "cathexis," "compulsive and psychopathic syndromes," and the like. He then proceeds to such statements as: "A *social system* is *motivated* as truly as an individual human being. . . . If a *political system* has *delusions* of omnipotence, this is likely . . . ," etc. (italics added).[19]

Personification and attribution of psychological characters to social systems, the state in particular, are widely and stoutly defended as a sort of verbal shorthand that saves time and type and deceives nobody. It is also defended sometimes as a positive contribution to the understanding of political systems. Kaplan, from whom we quoted just above, asserts further that "if . . . the specific action content is removed and they are treated in terms of the routing of information within the system, the various psychological mechanisms are isomorphic with mechanisms manifested in the behavior of social organizations." [20]

That the idiom of state personality saves time and type, no one could possibly deny. For this reason alone, speakers and writers will undoubtedly continue this usage. But it is just as certain that such usage tends to evoke reified images of the state. When Kaplan says that social structures are "isomorphic" with psycho-neural structures of

[18] R. A. North *et al.*, *Content Analysis: A Handbook with Applications for the Study of International Crises*, Northwestern University Press, 1963, pp. 147-48.
[19] M. A. Kaplan, *System and Process in International Politics*, Wiley, 1957, especially pp. 253*ff.*
[20] *Ibid.*, p. 253.

biological organisms, he is making an assertion to be empirically demonstrated, not uttering a self-evident axiom to be uncritically accepted as true. That even a purely metaphorical extension of human psychological characters to noncorporeal abstractions entails important consequences, moral and civic as well as purely intellectual, has been repeatedly recognized and emphasized by philosophers, historians, psychologists, and political scientists.[21]

Verbal personification leads easily (and apparently almost irresistibly) to the practice of ascribing to the state

[21] The philosopher T. D. Weldon says, of the attribution of human-like personality to the state, that "even as metaphors they are unsafe. . . ." *The Vocabulary of Politics,* Penguin, 1953, p. 48. The historian P. T. Moon argues the thesis that "language often obscures truth. More than is ordinarily realized, our eyes are blinded to the facts of international relations by tricks of the tongue. When one uses the simple monosyllable *France* one thinks of France as a unity, an entity. . . . [We] impute not only unity but also personality to the country. The very words conceal the facts and make international relations a glamorous drama in which personalized nations are the actors, and all too easily we forget the flesh-and-blood men and women who are the true actors." *Imperialism and World Politics,* Macmillan, 1926, p. 58. The psychologist Floyd Allport makes the same point: "This metaphor of the institution as a superhuman agency tends to pass over from mere convenience of usage to a literal and emotional acceptance. . . . Because of such personification, acts and qualities are ascribed to institutions in a way which is peculiarly misleading." *Institutional Behavior,* University of North Carolina Press, 1933, p. 478. Finally, to quote but one more of the many who have emphasized the consequences of personifying social systems, these words from Vernon Van Dyke: "Sometimes reification seems to be involved. That is, some references to the state seem to predicate the real existence of an entity quite apart from the human beings (the office-holders and others) who are the visible actors; perhaps it will be called an organism with a life and will of its own, existing independently of the life and will of the human beings who compose it. In view of the distinction of some of the writers who have seemed to reify the state in this way, it is perhaps better not to call the practice obvious nonsense. Yet there is nothing to say in support of the view, and there are many dangers in it." *Political Science: A Philosophical Analysis,* Stanford University Press, 1960, pp. 63-64.

the will and purposefulness, the emotional drives and psychological processes, which are the exclusive attributes of human organisms. Despite, perhaps because of, this tendency, theorists continue to build models of political systems in which the *state* is treated as an *environed unit capable of responding in human-like ways.*

Such usage poses an issue that becomes particularly refractory as soon as environmental terms and sentences are introduced. In what sense can one say that a state—a disembodied, invisible, noncorporeal abstraction—"envisages" ends (purposes, goals) and means (strategies, policies)? In what sense can one say that environing conditions "influence" or otherwise "affect" such an abstract entity? Indeed, in what sense can one speak of *state behavior* at all?

We place "envisage," "influence," and "affect" within quotation marks, because such transitive verbs connote instrumental connections, mechanisms, or processes of relationship. So far as we are able to determine, it is possible to establish empirical linkage between environing factors and psychological events (moods, attitudes, cognition, choices, decisions, etc.) only via the phenomena of apperception, phenomena observed only in concrete human individuals. This premise, we repeat, poses a most troublesome issue when the political "actor" is conceived to be an abstract entity.

One way out is to redefine the units of international politics—the states that comprise the society of nations—in a manner compatible with psychological modes of speaking. This solution is one of the salient features of the scheme for analyzing foreign policy, formulated early in the 1950's by R. C. Snyder and several associates. By equating state-action with the action of the state's human agents, they bypassed the difficulties inherent in state personification. From this perspective, the state becomes "its official decision-makers. . . . State action is the action taken by those acting in the name of the state." And there "can be no state action or reaction except as the decision-makers act and react." [22]

Whatever disadvantages from other standpoints may be entailed in this way of bypassing the troublesome concept of state personality, it helps decidedly to bring into manageable posture the relationship of environing conditions and events to foreign policy and to the processes of policy making. As long as the state *itself* is treated as a human-like entity, endowed with capacity to think, feel, perceive, desire, choose, and decide, it is difficult to make any sensible statements about the relations of environing factors to *state*-decisions.

It may often be impossible to identify the specific human agents who act in the name of the state, or to learn much that is relevant about their specific psychological reactions to environing conditions and events. This is a limiting feature of all foreign-policy analysis. But this limitation is not overcome in the slightest by substituting abstractions for concrete human actors. At the very least, we repeat, forms of expression that attribute action to human persons, rather than to intangible corporate entities, focus attention on the psychological phenomena (perception, cognition, communication, reasoning, choice, and all the rest) which alone provide any demonstrable instrumental linkage between environmental conditions and events and the processes of formulating national policies and strategies.

A related difficulty arises with reference both to the abstraction *state* and the still more abstract concept *system*. Environment (milieu) and environed unit are concepts

[22] R. C. Snyder *et al., Foreign Policy Decision Making,* Free Press, 1962, p. 65; E. S. Furniss, Jr., and R. C. Snyder, *An Introduction to American Foreign Policy,* Rinehart, 1955, p. 5.

with strong spatial connotations in the scientific fields from which political theorists have borrowed them. If one elects to speak of the international system's "environment," the system's "environmental capacity," and the "environmental constraints" on the system, in what sense is he speaking? [23] In what sense can a set of intangible social patterns be environed? A social system is neither a physical entity nor a biological organism. Then how can one speak of such a system having an environment? What precisely is environed by what? And what is the instrumental mechanism of relationship between milieu and unit? Is it sensible at all to employ ecological concepts and theories with reference to such abstractions?

These questions are not put frivolously. They reflect concern as to whether those who incorporate environmental terminology into system theories, and who speak of "environmental constraints" operating on the system, have given sufficient consideration to the troublesome issues of relationship which their usage poses. We shall return to this issue in the final chapter. Here we may simply note that it is not necessary to use environmental terminology at high levels of abstraction. For example, Quincy Wright has built a model of the international system upon concepts of "geographical and analytical fields," and thereby has bypassed most of the difficulties inherent in adapting ecological terminology to analytic constructs. [24]

If one elects to treat the state as the acting unit, but ascribes to it a more tangible entity (implicit in such terms as

[23] See, for example, R. N. Rosecrance, *Actions and Reaction in World Politics*, Little, Brown, 1964, especially index entries: "environmental constraints," and "environmental theory." For a more general discussion, see David Easton, "An Approach to the Analysis of Political Systems," in *World Politics*, 1957, v. 9, pp. 383*ff.*

[24] Quincy Wright, *The Study of International Relations*, Appleton-Century-Crofts, 1955, ch. 32, especially pp. 540*ff.*

country, nation, or political community), other technical issues emerge. If the state is treated as an entity in space, then technically only conditions and events external to the state's geographical boundaries can be included in its milieu. All that exists or occurs inside its geographic space is either ignored or treated as features of the state's internal structure and functions, remotely analogous perhaps to the bodily structures and functions of a biological organism.

Some systems theorists seem to postulate the state as a sort of hard-shell entity, responsive only to stimuli coming from outside the shell—that is, from outside the state's geographic space. This seems to be substantially the position, for example, of the political theorist Arthur Burns. In an essay on international politics, Burns denies the relevance of the behavioral sciences to the study of international politics, on the ground that the state's internal structure and the characteristics of its human agents are largely irrelevant, or at least only marginally relevant, as compared with threats and other stimuli originating outside the state's geographic space.[25]

Others seem to postulate the state as the environed unit, and then to treat phenomena inside the state's geographic space as if these too were factors of the state's milieu. When this is done, there would appear to be implicit reference to two kinds of environed units, employed interchangeably and without specification: in some contexts, the state as a corporate entity; in others, some human agent or set of human agents of the state.

If one elects to identify the government of the state as the unit of action, then the concept of milieu expands by definition to include not only phenomena outside the state's geographic space, but also nongovernmental phenomena inside that space as well. If, as Snyder and others

[25] A. L. Burns, "From Balance to Deterrence," in *World Politics,* 1957, v. 9, pp. 494, 496.

have done, the state itself is redefined (for analytical purposes) in terms of its concrete human agents (see page 37, above), the content of the milieu enlarges still further to include conditions and events external to the specific decision makers within the governmental organization, who are identified as speaking with authority for the state.

We have previously stated (page 32, above) that it may or may not be of practical consequence whether particular phenomena are classified as structures of the environed unit or as factors of its milieu. It definitely does matter, if verbal classification (as in the Burns model cited above) has the effect of structuring analysis so as to divert attention from factors which, from a different analytical perspective, might appear to be quite significant.[26] How one draws the line between unit and milieu also has practical as well as purely analytic consequences, depending on whether the focus is on *psychological behavior* or on achievement or accomplishment as measured in terms of *capabilities*.

[26] Attention has been given to the analytic puzzle of how to conceive an environment for the global international system, an abstraction derived from political patterns that, in the aggregate, are coterminous with the earth's surface. F. W. Riggs resolves this puzzle by characterizing the "international system [as] a power structure in which the weight of external pressures approaches the vanishing point"—that is, a system that has no environment. "International Relations as a Prismatic System," in *The International System: Theoretical Essays*, edited by Klaus Knorr and Sidney Verba, Princeton University Press, 1962, p. 151. To this solution, C. F. Alger objects that such an "analytic posture may inhibit our comprehension of potentially significant aspects of international relations." Alger solves this puzzle by abstracting from the aggregate of global phenomena those patterns that exhibit an international political quality, calling these latter the international system, and treating all the rest as the environment of the inernational system. "Comparisons of Intranational and International Politics," in *American Political Science Review*, 1963, v. 57, pp. 407ff. This solution is ingenious, but a less scholastic (and in our view, prefer-

FOCAL TERMS AND CONCEPTS

Psycho-ecological concepts (the milieu as perceived and reacted to) and theories of cognition, motivation, and decision-making will not work at all at the level of systems theory. This is so because it is purely metaphorical to attribute psychological characters to such abstract entities as the state, the political system, or the international system. It is inescapably metaphorical, we repeat, because abstract entities are not biological organisms, and do not resemble such organisms in any behavioral sense. Psycho-ecological concepts and theories, formulated with reference to human persons, as individuals or in concrete groups, simply make no sense whatever when applied to political systems or other high-level abstractions.

For reasons which we shall now touch upon briefly, and to which we shall return later (in Chapter X), environmental concepts and theories present less difficulty when applied to organizations *in the context of performance and the capabilities upon which performance depends*. In explaining past performance, or in predicting future performance, the task is not limited to examining the psychological behavior of the unit's human agents. The task is rather to identify and evaluate those structures and properties, *both* of the unit and of its milieu, that set limits to what is (or may be) accomplished in *given* contingencies with reference to *given* goals and strategies.

This statement holds for a game, or a voyage, or a business venture, or a government's operations, or any other undertaking. As we shall show later (in Chapters V, VIII, and IX), environmental limitations on performance extend beyond cognition and may be operative irrespective of the cognition of the environed unit (be it a single individual, a concrete human group, or the human members of a corporate entity). For example, one can make many sen-

able) solution would be simply to describe the international system in terms of limiting variables, without use of ecological terms at all.

sible statements about the performance of a football team
(which may be conceived as a social system) without in-
voking *psycho*-ecological terms and theories at all. One can
characterize the style of play and account for the team's
victories and defeats without going into the psychological
reasons why the quarterback or the coach ordered particular sequences of plays. But the moment attention is directed to this latter issue, the analyst must move from the
system level to the human-actor level in order to formulate
psychologically sensible explanations.

Thus far we have repeatedly spoken of man-milieu *relationships* without attempting to specify what such relationships may involve. In anticipation of what is to follow
in later chapters, it may be noted here that we shall be concerned mainly with the following aspects of relationship:
(1) observed regularities between variables (expressed as
correlations or associations); and (2) general hypotheses
that purport to establish the instrumental means (mechanisms, processes, etc.) which account satisfactorily for observed regularities. From the ecological perspective, such
explanatory hypotheses divide into two categories: (a)
those that purport to explain connections between environmental factors and psychological phenomena (values and
preferences, moods and attitudes, perception and apperception, cognition and recognition, modes of deliberating,
framing alternatives, and making decisions, etc.); and (2)
hypotheses that purport to identify and explain the level
of achievement or performance of a specified environed
unit with reference to a *given* undertaking. With respect
to any of the above, relational statements may be framed
in terms of necessity (for example, where C, there E; or,
in the absence of C, no E), or they may be framed in
terms of some degree of probability (where C, probably
E, etc.). Probabilistic statements may represent a tidy statistical mean of a large aggregate of events, calculated with

or without regard to volition; or they may represent untidy assumptions or expectations intuitively derived from the cumulative experiences of daily living.

All these ideas of relationship stand in contrast to the agnostic posture towards relationships and explanations still encountered, though less than formerly, among students of human affairs. Since the agnostic posture poses an issue of considerable importance to our whole discussion, we propose to say a few more words about it, even at some risk of being accused of whipping a dead (or dying) horse.

The agnostic posture towards explanation, so-called pure empiricism, has been encountered in the social disciplines most frequently among historians and geographers, though plenty of political scientists have exhibited addiction, too. A geographer describes an industrial layout, or an areal distribution of crops, or a transportation grid, or some other geographical pattern. A historian presents a chronicle of events. A political scientist describes a governmental structure or process. In each instance, the speaker may avoid, or try to avoid, expressing judgments as to how or why things happen thus and so—more specifically, as to how the human actors upon the stage are connected with the properties of the stage or with other aspects of the milieu in which they are operating. It is as if one were to report that most farmers grow corn in Iowa and raise cattle in Wyoming, and were then to assert his inability to explain why, or to disclaim any interest in trying to do so. Symptoms of this disease are such statements as "Let's stick to the facts," or "Let the facts speak for themselves."

To such statements one replies, of course, that the facts *never* speak for themselves. Even the purest description or chronology includes implicit interpretation. No one can report everything. What one observes and records, what he retains and discards, how he arranges the data he calls "facts," all reflect judgments as to what he considers to be relevant and significant. By the very act of selecting and ordering his data, and by the verbal or other symbols which he chooses in presenting them, the "pure" empiricist explains, interprets, and theorizes, protestations to the contrary notwithstanding. As a famous economist is said to have observed, "The most vicious theorists are those who claim to let the facts speak for themselves."

Our point, to repeat, is that it is impossible to answer the questions of "what" and "where" with respect to any complex course of events or state of affairs, without becoming involved to some degree with questions of "how" and "why." The moment these questions are admitted, even if only by implication, the speaker introduces some hypothesis of relationship between the actor and his milieu.

A wholly different question is what constitutes a *satisfactory* explanation of such relationships. Various kinds of answers have been given to this question, a question that underlies every one of the explanatory hypotheses to be considered in later chapters.[27] At this point we merely take notice that, in common speech, explanation consists ordinarily of answering questions that begin with "why," and that such sentences usually take the form of a statement of cause-and-effect.

Causality, it might be noted, is firmly built into our language, and into many (but not all) other languages as well. It is difficult to think or to communicate without recourse to causal verbs—influence, affect, determine, control, compel, coerce, prevent, produce, push, pull, press, and hundreds of others. Such verbs link a causal agent (the gram-

[27] There is a large and very technical literature on the nature of explanation. Some of this literature is cited later, in Chapter VIII, especially page 143.

matical subject of the sentence) with an affected result (the grammatical object).[28]

Cause-and-effect rhetoric is often combined with teleological idioms. "Nature" is said to push man this way and that, and the like. We shall return to this semantic issue, with its important ecological implications, when we come to examine environmental determinism and its watered-down derivative, free-will environmentalism.

Application of concepts and theories derived from the physical sciences has recently put the relationship issue into slightly different perspective. The physicist J. Q. Stewart and the geographer William Warntz provoked a minor tempest when they applied certain "laws" of physical science to "explain" various "macrodistributions of social phenomena in space." They hypothesized, among other things, that the influence of an aggregate of people is proportional to their number, divided by their distance away from the point where their influence is measured.[29]

[28] This aspect of linguistics has drawn considerable attention and comment in recent years. The words one uses and the ways he puts them together affect his images both of reality and of relations to his milieu. The geographer David Lowenthal contends that "the structural aspects of language influence ways of looking at the world more than do vocabularies. Seldom consciously employed, usually slow to change, syntax pervades basic modes of thought. . . . [For example] lacking transitive verbs, Greenlanders tend to see things happen without specific cause; 'I kill him,' in their language, becomes 'he dies to me.' In European tongues, however, action accompanies perception, and the transitive verb animates every event with purpose and cause." "Geography, Experience, and Imagination: Towards a Geographical Epistemology," in *Annals, Association of American Geographers*, 1961, v. 51, pp. 241, 254-55. Lowenthal cites many of the authorities on this much-neglected aspect of man-milieu relationship theory.

[29] See J. Q. Stewart, *Coasts, Waves and Weather*, Ginn, 1945, pp. 163-65; Stewart, "Natural Law Factors in United States Foreign Policy," in *Social Science*, 1954, v. 3, pp. 137ff; Stewart and Warntz, "Macrogeography and Social Science," in *Geographical Review*, 1958, v. 48, pp. 167ff; Warntz, "Geography at Mid-

FOCAL TERMS AND CONCEPTS

The Stewart-Warntz formula, or rule, or law, is a generalized statement of certain man-milieu relationships. Does it thereby constitute a satisfactory explanation of the relationships in question? Or does it merely identify an association, or pattern, in space, in a manner which leaves the "why" question hanging unanswered? As a generalized statement of relations among variables, the formula meets the specification of a theory, as generally understood in science. Is a theory, confirmed or unconfirmed, equivalent to an explanation? We shall return to these questions after examining various philosophical postures towards man-milieu relationships, and the frames of analysis and argument into which these postures are cast.

These postures towards the man-milieu relationship issue are designated respectively: environmental determinism, free-will environmentalism, possibilism, probabilistic behavioralism, and cognitive behavioralism. These are not very tidy categories. They are neither conceptually parallel nor quite mutually exclusive. But these labels do identify recognized postures towards man-milieu relationships.[80] We shall examine them textually and critically. We shall then reconsider them all in the light of more general aspects of explanation and prediction, with a view to establishing, if possible, a generally consistent, logically tenable, and more fruitful mode of thinking about man-milieu relationships.

Twentieth Century," in *World Politics,* 1959, v. 11, pp. 442*ff;* Warntz, "A New Map of the Surface of Population Potentials for the United States, 1960," in *Geographical Review,* 1964, v. 54, pp. 170*ff.*

[80] In the earlier version of this essay we called these postures *hypotheses.* They are hypotheses in the general sense that each identifies a particular mode of formulating a certain class of relationships. But *hypothesis* in this broad general sense should be differentiated from *hypothesis* in the narrower sense of a tentative topical statement of relationships among variables.

3

ENVIRONMENTAL DETERMINISM

DETERMINISM IS a well-known philosophical doctrine. It appears in different forms in different contexts. The essence of the doctrine, as generally understood, is simply that *all* empirical phenomena of the system under consideration (be it a mechanical, biological, or social system) can be predicted by reference to some set of causal laws. Thus a determinist might postulate that all human behavior and achievement are determined by reference to limits set by the hereditary characters and by the milieu of the individual under consideration. If our hypothetical determinist then assumes hereditary characters to be constant parameters through the time-span with which he is concerned, he comes to the posture that human behavior can be predicted by reference to variables in the individual's milieu.

In practice, strict environmental determinism has generally referred to the thesis that some set of environmental factors, less than the total milieu, is sufficient to account for, or to provide a firm basis for predicting, both the psychological behavior of human beings and the empirical outcomes of their undertakings. Applied rigorously, this philosophical posture envisages man as a sort of chip in the stream of history. He is borne along by a current which he is incapable of resisting, within a channel from which he cannot escape. Man may imagine himself to be free to choose. But in the view of the strict environmental determinist, environing conditions actually dictate his so-called choices; and hence man really has no capacity for choice in any meaningful sense.

From this perspective, a human being is not essentially

different from an acorn. The acorn falls to the ground. If it is fertile and if it encounters favorable conditions of moisture, temperature, light, etc., one can predict that the acorn will develop into a seedling oak. So far as anyone knows, the acorn has no choice in the matter. Its behavior varies autonomically within the limits set by its hereditary characters and its environment. If heredity is assumed to be constant, we repeat, both the initiation of acorn-behavior and the resulting state-of-acorn-affairs are explicable and predictable by reference to the relevant factors of the acorn's environment.

Whether the limits set by man's hereditary character and by his total milieu do in fact leave any room for volition, whether in any ultimate sense man has a free will, we assume to be unknowable. In fact, environmental determinists rarely pose the issue in this manner. What they usually claim, or appear to assume, is that either man's total milieu, or more commonly some set of environmental factors less than totality—as, for example, the factors of climate—suffices to explain satisfactorily and to predict with reasonable certainty both the tasks which he initiates and any state-of-affairs that results therefrom.

So much for philosophical generalities! When one comes to analyze discourse which appears at first glance to reflect environmental deterministic thinking, he uncovers a semantic state of affairs that can fairly be called chaotic. Among other possible variants, one will discover:

1st, a varied assortment of loosely impressionistic, generally teleological interpretations, in which human history is explained in terms of physical environmental "causes";

2nd, interpretations of history derived from rather more rigorous correlations observed in space and through time between a social patterns and certain nonhuman factors;

3rd, innumerable exhibits of deterministic and near-deterministic rhetoric which do not, when read in context, appear to confirm a philosophical commitment to environmental determinism;

4th, explicit assertions of such a commitment in contexts which simultaneously appear to posit freedom of choice in particular cases;

5th, discourse in which the hypothesis of environmental determinism is asserted to posit 100 per cent predictability, and hence inferentially a denial of volition;

6th, discourse in which determinism is conceived in statistical terms as a degree of regularity, in large aggregates of events, sufficient to formulate rules for predicting on the average within some calculable margin of error.

One could cite a great many exhibits of the impressionistic variety of environmental determinism. Numerous passages in the classics of political philosophy, Montesquieu in particular, have been construed this way.[1] The English historian Thomas Buckle, writing in mid-nineteenth century, penned many statements such as the following: ". . . in India, slavery, abject, eternal slavery, was the natural state of the great body of the people; it was the state to which they were *doomed by physical laws utterly impossible to resist*" (italics added).[2]

One can find in the writings of the German geographer Friedrich Ratzel such statements as: "The course of history in America, just as in corresponding periods of time in northern Asia, in Africa, and in Australia, only confirms the belief that lands, no matter how distant from one another they may be, whenever their climates are similar, are destined to be scenes of analogous historical development."[3]

[1] For example, Book XIV, of *L'Esprit des Lois,* in which Montesquieu discussed the effects of climate on human capabilities.

[2] H. T. Buckle, *History of Civilization in England,* World's Classics edition, 1903, v. 1, p. 59.

[3] From "Man as a Life Phenomenon on the Earth," in *The*

ENVIRONMENTAL DETERMINISM

Ellen Churchill Semple, one of Ratzel's distinguished pupils, likewise made many assertions which, if literally construed, appear to reflect sheer impressionistic environmental determinism. For example, discussing the "interplay of the *forces* of land and sea," she contended: "In some cases a small, infertile, niggardly country *conspires* with a *beckoning* sea to *drive* its sons out upon the deep; in others, a wide territory with a generous soil *keeps* its well-fed children at home and *silences* the *call* of the sea" (italics added).[4]

At the close of the nineteenth century, the French historian Edmond Demolins posed the question: "Il existe à la surface du globe terrestre une infinie variété des populations; quelle est la cause qui a créé cette variété?"

To this question, Demolins gave the following answer: "la route que les peuples ont suivie"—meaning by "route" not only the lands and areas traversed by migrating peoples but also the character of the places where they settled and lived. He continued: "C'est la route qui crée la race et qui crée le type social. Les routes du globe ont été en quelque sorte des alambics puissants, qui ont transformé, de telle manière ou de telle autre, les peuples qui s'y sont engagés. . . .

"Modifiez l'une ou l'autre de ces routes, élevez-la, ou abaissez-la, faites-y pousser telle production au lieu de telle autre, transformez ainsi dans tel sens ou dans tel autre la forme et la nature du travail, aussitôt le type social est modifié et vous obtenez une autre race.

"Je vais plus loin: *si l'histoire de l'humanité recommençait, sans que la surface du globe ait été transformée, cette histoire se répéterait dans ses grandes lignes.* Il y aurait bien des différences secondaires . . .

World's History, edited by H. F. Helmolt, London, 1901, v. 1, p. 64.
  [4] *Influences of Geographic Environment*, Holt, 1911, p. 15.

mais les mêmes routes reproduiraient les mêmes types sociaux, et leur imposeraient les mêmes caractères essentiels" (italics added).[5]

Examples of impressionistic environmental determinism could be extended indefinitely. In the main, they represent loose generalizations from scattered observations. Though human volition is rarely denied, the impression generally conveyed is that human aspirations and undertakings as well as human accomplishments are somehow determined by nonhuman conditions and events. Thus history is the record of human successes and failures to adapt to opportunities and obstacles present in the physical habitat of the society under consideration.

"In every problem of history [Semple wrote] there are two main factors, variously stated as heredity and environment, man and his geographic conditions, the internal forces of race and the external forces of habitat. Now the geographic element in the long history of human development has been operating strongly and operating persistently. Herein lies its importance. It is a stable force. It never sleeps. This natural environment, this physical basis of history, is for all intents and purposes immutable in comparison with the other factor in the problem—shifting, plastic, progressive, retrogressive man." [6]

This passage seems to us to reflect a state of mind implicit in much of the impressionistic environmental determinism of the nineteenth and earlier centuries: a deeply rooted sense of human dependence upon a physical habitat largely beyond human ability to alter or control. This theme comes through even more strongly in the writings of some of Semple's contemporaries and predeces-

[5] *Les grandes routes des peuples: Essai de géographie sociale,* Paris, 1901, v. 1, pp. vii, ix.

[6] E. C. Semple, *Influences of Geographic Environment,* Holt, 1911, p. 2.

sors. One of these was the Oxford historian-geographer H. B. George. In a now all-but-forgotten little book, first published in 1901, George dwelt on the "influence" of the earth on preindustrial peoples: ". . . the less they knew [about the earth and about the tools and skills necessary to shape it to their ends], the more influence geography was likely to have over their destinies. . . . We need always to remember this, in attempting to estimate the bearings of geography on history. If we could imagine the possibility of mankind in general having known, throughout human history, what is now known of the earth's surface, the course of that history might have been very materially altered." [7]

As C. L. Glacken and others have emphasized, one of the consequences of the accelerating advance of technology in the nineteenth and twentieth centuries has been a corresponding increase in the capacity of the technically more advanced societies to alter and control their physical environment.[8] But ancient ideas often outlive changing reality. Also it is easy to forget, in the 1960's, how very recently (within the memory of millions), even in the technically most advanced countries, people were dangerously vulnerable to the vicissitudes of Nature. Perhaps (and here we are admittedly speculating), in far greater degree than is generally appreciated in our time, it was some such sense of dependence that inspired the impressionistic determinism of Semple, some of her contemporaries, and those who phrased similar ideas in earlier centuries.

A more tightly reasoned brand of environmental deter-

[7] H. B. George, *The Relations of Geography and History,* Oxford, 1901; 5th and last edition, 1924, p. 5.
[8] See Chapter V, below; also C. L. Glacken, "Changing Ideas of the Habitable World," in *Man's Role in Changing the Face of the Earth,* edited by W. L. Thomas, Jr., University of Chicago Press, 1956, pp. 70, 86.

minism—*quasi-determinism* would be more precisely accurate—came in with the investigations and writings of Ellsworth Huntington. During the first half of this century, Huntington was certainly the most notable, perhaps the most controversial, figure in the continuing debate over man-milieu relationships. In a long succession of books and essays, he supported the thesis that climatic variations in space and through time determine both the geographical distributions of "civilization" in any period, and also the rise and decline of civilizations through historical time.

Huntington assembled and deployed a formidable mass of data, some of it statistical, about the geographical distribution of health and disease, literacy and education, birthplaces of famous people, ownership of automobiles, and a great many other indices of "general progress." He collected evidence of climatic changes in cyclic patterns through the centuries; and he correlated the rise and decline of civilizations with these climatic cycles.

Huntington's climatic hypothesis is summed up in the following short quotations:

His major premise: ". . . a certain type of climate prevails wherever civilization is high. In the past the same type seems to have prevailed wherever a great civilization arose." [9]

His derived hypothesis: "Whether we turn to Civil Service Examinations, the use of liquor, business fluctuations, immigration, or crops, climatic conditions are in one way or another a variable factor *upon which variations in the others depend*" (italics added).[10]

The political implication: "The expansion of the great

[9] Huntington, *Civilization and Climate*, Yale University Press, 1915, p. 24.

[10] Huntington, *World Power and Evolution*, Yale University Press, 1919, p. 186.

nations of the world is to a large extent determined by climatic conditions." [11]

Huntington repeatedly qualified his generalizations. He cited the limitations imposed by man's biological heredity and also by what he called the "cultural environment." [12] Despite such qualifying statements, however, the geographer O. H. K. Spate concluded, after careful study, that climate was the factor that really made the difference for Huntington. [13] Others have disputed this conclusion. S. S. Visher, one of Huntington's scholarly collaborators, who knew him intimately, has insisted that Huntington was not an "extreme environmentalist," and that he was always "keenly aware that the physical environment generally is of secondary or indirect significance. . . ." [14]

One cannot resolve this issue by quoting texts. So much depends on which passages one chooses to emphasize! More important, in our view, is the impetus that Huntington's powerful intellect gave to further theorizing along this line in mid-twentieth century.

One thus inspired has been the psychologist R. H. Wheeler. Investigating historical rhythms in patterns of human behavior, Wheeler blundered into the discovery of correlations between those rhythms and the climatic changes reflected in the growth rings of the sequoia trees in California. This discovery led him to Huntington, who had used this evidence in support of his hypothesis of climatic change. Wheeler's project, which had started

[11] *Ibid.*, p. 24.
[12] See, for example, *Civilization and Climate*, p. 9; also his *Mainsprings of Civilization*, Wiley, 1945, pp. 8-9.
[13] Spate, "Toynbee and Huntington: A Study in Determinism," in *Geographical Journal*, London, 1952, v. 118, pp. 406ff.
[14] S. S. Visher, "Ellsworth Huntington, Human Ecologist," in *Journal of Human Ecology*, 1952, v. 2, No. 1, p. 7.

within the province of Gestalt psychology, became a major investigation in historical geography.

Wheeler has reported discovery of remarkably consistent correlations since the dawn of history between climatic cycles and recurrent wars, revolutions, and other political and social events. He is convinced that "intensive study of the climate of the past will ultimately lead to accurate predictions of trends far ahead into the future, and that the climatic phases of the future will probably produce the same types of cultural and behavioral problems as they seem to have produced in the past, over and over again, *by controlling man's vitality and energy level*" (italics added).[15]

C. A. Mills (professor emeritus of the Cincinnati University Medical School) has added another dimension to Huntington's and Wheeler's theses. Mills has not only observed human behavior in varied climates; he has also buttressed these observations by extensive experiments with laboratory animals, and by marshaling well-known facts about human physiology.[16]

Mills takes off from the phenomena of human metabolism. He likens our bodies to inefficient internal combustion engines. We take in fuel in the form of food, and our bodies transform some of it into useful work-energy. But for every unit so utilized, the human body must get rid of "three or four units" as "waste heat." This is accomplished by evaporation of sweat and other well-understood physical and physiological processes. These processes are affected by air temperature, relative humidity,

[15] R. H. Wheeler, "Climate and Human Behavior," in *Encyclopaedia of Psychology*, edited by P. L. Harriman, Philosophical Library, 1946, p. 86; and Wheeler, *War, 559 B.C.—1950 A.D.*, Foundation for the Study of Cycles, 1951.

[16] Mills's work is reported in the respected magazine *Science*, organ of the American Association for the Advancement of Science, September 16, 1949, v. 110, pp. 267*ff*.

circulation, and other atmospheric variables. The human organism can adapt only within quite narrow limits of variation. Prolonged exposure to extreme cold, heat, dampness, or other unfavorable conditions depresses the individual's initiative, learning capacity, memory recall, reasoning ability, and may even destroy his organism prematurely.[17]

In these physio-psychic responses Mills finds confirmation of Huntington's hypothesis that climate embraces the set of environing factors which largely determine the geographical distribution and the level of human accomplishment. From rather precise experiments with laboratory animals, Mills shifts to a less precise interpretation of history, couched in prose reminiscent of the deterministic rhetoric so popular half a century earlier.

In certain regions, according to Mills, temperature "lays a heavy, stagnating hand over [man's] life and holds him to a vegetable existence. . . ." In other regions, more favorable climate "generates an energy and progressiveness which drives him forward with irresistible impetus. . . . Man is . . . a pawn of the environmental forces encompassing him." Looking to the future, he accepts the hypothesis that we are in the midst of a centurylong warming-up period. This has brought to the temperate zone "definitely milder winters and the long summers of depressive heat that sap human energy and change the course of nations." These conditions are "creeping northward over the United States and Central Europe." But farther to the north, the Soviet Union, occupying a region long retarded by "benumbing winter cold," now

[17] Mills's physiological findings are confirmed in the main, and considerably extended, by much more elaborate experiments on human subjects, conducted in the Laboratory of Hygiene at Yale University, and reported in C. E. A. Winslow and L. P. Harrington, *Temperature and Human Life*, Princeton University Press, 1949, especially pp. 252ff.

rides the climatic wave of the future, with much of its vast territory enjoying atmospheric conditions that are "near the optimal for human endeavor."

Mills employs much deterministic rhetoric. It is easy to conclude that he is a convinced environmental determinist, that he believes that climatic factors, temperature patterns in particular, account for the geographical distribution of political power and for the rise and decline of nations and civilizations.[18]

However, like Huntington, Wheeler, and most other apparent environmental determinists, Mills guards his line of retreat. The strict determinist finds in the milieu as a whole, or in some set of environmental factors, the "sufficient cause" *both* of human undertakings *and* of the complex states-of-affairs associated therewith. But Mills and Wheeler explicitly, and Huntington implicitly, concentrate mainly on the human organism's *capacity* for achievement. They do not contend that climate compels men to choose one goal rather than another. They simply try to demonstrate that climate sets a ceiling, or outer limit, on human capacity to achieve whatever goal is selected. If this is a correct reading, their conclusions with respect to human capabilities (stripped of deterministic rhetoric) could be expressed as well or better in terms of the philosophical posture commonly called environmental possibilism (to be taken up in Chapter V).

In the social sciences generally, and especially in human geography, environmental determinism has long been under heavy attack.[19] Yet deterministic figures of

[18] For a fuller statement of Mills's thesis, see his earlier book, *Climate Makes the Man*, Harper, 1942. For a critical commentary, see A. Missenard, *A la recherche de l'homme*, Librairie Istia, Paris, 1954, part 3: "Climat et milieu physique." English translation, *In Search of Man*, Hawthorn Books, 1957, part 3, "Climate and Physical Environment."

[19] See, for example, Isaiah Bowman, *Geography in Relation to*

ENVIRONMENTAL DETERMINISM

speech persist tenaciously in the literature of geography
and the social sciences. Consider, for example, Sir Halford Mackinder's often-quoted maxim: "Who rules East
Europe commands the Heartland; who rules the Heartland commands the World-Island; who rules the World-
Island commands the World." [20] Or E. W. Zimmerman's
statement that the Thomas-Gilchrist process for making
steel out of acidic iron ores, such as those of Alsace-Lor-
raine, *"led inevitably* to Germany's industrial hegemony
on the continent" of Europe (italics added).[21] Or the cat-
egorical assertion by the historian T. A. Bailey that "geography *led inexorably* to the adoption" of the early United
States policy of avoiding alliances with European powers
(italics added).[22] Or, to cite one more example, the following passage from a textbook on the history of seapower: "England, *driven* to the sea by her sparse resources to seek a livelihood and to find homes for her
burgeoning population, and sitting athwart the main sea
routes of Western Europe, *seemed destined by geography
to command the seas"* (italics added).[23]

Sometimes speakers lapse into deterministic rhetoric
after explicitly rejecting deterministic causation. Thus, for
example, the authors of a certain textbook repudiate environmental determinism, state their theme as "man's adjustment to his natural environment"—and then proceed

the Social Sciences, Scribner, 1934, p. 69; and R. S. Platt, "Determinism in Geography," in *Annals,* Association of American
Geographers, 1948, v. 38, pp. 126ff. Many other critiques could
be cited.
    [20] H. J. Mackinder, *Democratic Ideals and Reality,* Holt, 1942
edition, p. 150.
    [21] *World Resources and Industries,* revised edition, Harper, 1951,
p. 648.
    [22] T. A. Bailey, *A Diplomatic History of the American People,*
2nd edition, Crofts, 1945, p. 7.
    [23] E. B. Potter *et al., The United States and World Sea Power,*
Prentice-Hall, 1955, p. 44.

to make such statements as: "civilization . . . has developed only in those parts of the world where a cold or a dry season . . . has *forced* man to produce a surplus for the dormant period" (italics added).[24]

Close reading in full context of such statements as these generally fails to confirm any rigorous environmental determinism at all. One should not minimize, however, the cumulative impact of deterministic rhetoric. There may be much wisdom in the old saw: "How do I know what I think until I hear what I say?" [25]

It may be of some interest to note that environmental determinism, or at least deterministic rhetoric, seems to persist most tenaciously with respect to that set of physical factors which to date man has shown the least capacity to control: namely, the weather. Perhaps this helps to account for the persistence of climatic determinism as manifested in the writings cited above. Also, without endorsing the extreme generalizations of some climatic determinists, one can note that there is a sense in which man's relation to the atmosphere differs from his relations to the distribution of earth materials, or to the layout of lands and seas. These latter are simply there, presenting at any given level of technology and other social conditions a latent set of opportunities and limitations which men may perceive and evaluate in various ways. The atmosphere, on the other hand, can produce direct effects on the human organism through physical discharge of energy.

Consider, for example, the behavior of a person sitting in a room in which the air temperature and the relative

[24] G. L. White and G. T. Renner, *Geography: An Introduction to Human Ecology*, Appleton-Century, 1936, p. 42.
[25] Metaphors slip imperceptibly "from mere convenience of usage to a literal and emotional acceptance." Floyd Allport, *Institutional Behavior*, University of North Carolina Press, 1933, p. 476.

humidity are gradually rising. His body responds in various ways to the change in environing conditions. These responses may include, among others, changes in body metabolism, rate of heartbeat, blood pressure, and body temperature. An observer might regard these events as purposeful behavior in the sense that they represent the organism's adjustments to environing changes which threaten its well-being or even survival. But as long as such adjustments stay below the individual's threshold of conscious perception, he is unaware of what is happening. Even when he becomes conscious of his bodily responses, there is little that he can do directly to alter them, so long as the environmental stimulus continues. Thus, with respect to a certain range of behavior, the human organism appears to respond just about as deterministically to environmental stimuli as does the acorn or other subhuman organisms.

What a person can do, how well he can do it, how long he can focus his attention, what he will want to do, and whether he will want to do anything at all, would thus appear to depend not only on his materials, tools, knowledge, and social organization. If the above argument is valid, the manner in which he carries on depends also on complex and at least partially autonomic bodily responses to external stimuli. Moreover, individuals differ considerably as to their so-called "normal" rates of metabolism and heartbeat, and their "normal" levels of blood pressure and body temperature. For these and perhaps other reasons as well, no two persons respond exactly alike to climatic stimuli.

What is salubrious for one may be depressing, even ruinous for another. An individual's conscious "feelings" may provide some clue to his bodily state. But just as often there appears to be little or no reliable correlation between a person's sense of comfort or discomfort and his ability to perform a given set of functions at any prescribed standard of efficiency, or to perform them as efficiently as someone else endowed with a different physiological set-up functioning under identical conditions.[26]

Now let us shift the setting, and consider other more or less autonomic adjustments to the milieu. A person may be habituated to a diet low in calories, or in proteins, or in vitamins, or deficient in other essential respects. Or he may be accustomed to a diet too rich in certain food elements. He may experience no conscious discomfort; or if he does, he may or may not associate it with these particular environmental factors. But his capacity for work and his *attitude towards work* may change significantly following improvement of his diet.

Now consider still another variant on this theme. A person may harbor parasites which interfere with his nutrition. Or he may suffer from debilitating diseases which deplete his blood or otherwise sap his vitality. He may or may not know how or why. Yet his energy and his psychic attitudes may profoundly change after eradication of the disturbing environmental factors.

Now let us shift the setting yet again. A man, walking in the dark, is struck down by an unseen assailant. Or a person is bitten by an unperceived snake. Or one is thrown from his bed by an earthquake or a bolt of lightning. In each case the human organism is responding nonvolitionally to stimuli from his milieu.

All the examples posed in the last few paragraphs seem to justify the conclusion that neither cognition nor volition, nor both together, are essential ingredients of *all*

[26] Nothing said here is intended to minimize man's ability, through increasing knowledge and improved technology, to achieve better adaptations by means of diet, clothing, exercise, chemotherapy, house-heating, air-cooling, etc.

behavioral relationships between man and his milieu. We would even venture to suggest, in the light of the above examples, that there seems to be at least a small range on the total spectrum of human behavior—including possibly some behavior highly relevant to the study of politics [27]—which is quite satisfactorily explicable in terms of a strict environmental determinism. That is to say, man's non-volitional responses to changes in the atmosphere, quantities and properties of foodstuffs eaten, invading parasites, bacteria and viruses, unperceived behavior of other persons or lower animals, inanimate discharges of energy in nature, etc., may conceivably set limits to human *choice* as well as these most assuredly do to human *capacities* for executing chosen projects.

In the examples cited, and in others that will come to mind, a discharge of energy in the milieu is the activating factor in the man-milieu relationships—precisely as posited in the chip-in-the-stream metaphor used at the beginning of this chapter. Is it not just possible that the precipitous retreat from environmental determinism which took place some decades ago in geography and in the social sciences generally, may be a case of the proverbial throwing out the baby with the bath-water?

Posing this question is not to be construed as a thinly disguised argument for restoring strict environmental determinism to the workshop of social analysis. Even if it appears that a certain range of human behavior is quite satisfactorily explicable in strictly deterministic terms, and even if it further appears that some of that behavior has significance for the problem in hand, it is still possible that environmental determinism offers a less acceptable mode

[27] From the standpoint of the stricken man and of those charged with guarding him, the assassination of President Kennedy was as non-volitional—as environmentally deterministic, if you will—as if the President had been struck by a bolt of lightning.

than some other, for explaining or predicting even the kinds of behavioral events and resulting states-of-affairs cited above. We shall return to this issue later when we come (in Chapter VI) to examine the probabilistic approach to man-milieu relationships.

Certain recent trends in international political analysis raise the issue of environmental determinism in slightly different form. We refer in particular to the development of concepts and theories about political systems. Some concept of system underlies every branch of organized knowledge. One speaks of the solar system, climatic systems, atoms and molecules as systems, plants and animals as biological systems. All sorts of man-made machines are conceived as mechanical systems. Sociologists analyze various kinds of social systems. System is also a familiar term in political discourse: for example, the American political system, democratic and communist systems, the historic European States System, the inter-American system, and many others.

All known concepts of system have a common core of meaning. This can be defined as a set of elements, or components, or units, which are observed to exist or to function in accordance with a discernible pattern. Beyond that, however, systemic concepts differ widely. A familiar concept in mechanical and biological systems is the self-regulating mechanism, called homeostasis. Many social theorists contend that something equivalent to homeostasis is observable in social systems. That is to say, many social systems appear to exhibit a propensity, when disturbed, to return to a former steady state. A family, a fraternal order, a political community, or other social group may penalize those of its members who deviate too widely from approved norms, standards, and values. Failure to check such deviation may destroy the group or transmute it into something quite different. For example, one can describe political revolutions in this way.

Somewhat similar is the idea of equilibrium through balanced power, an idea associated for several hundred years with political relations in the society of nations. When one state, or coalition of states, has become too strong or threateningly aggressive in the estimation of the rulers of other states, the latter have traditionally formed new alliances, strengthened their military forces, or taken other steps to restore a sort of equilibrium. Such behavior has recently been characterized as evidence of a homeostatic propensity in the international system.

Homeostasis may provide a suggestive analogy, but it also carries certain ecological connotations. It imparts to political theory a certain deterministic flavor: the notion of a mechanism or an organism operating *out of control of the human persons* who in an ultimate sense comprise the system.[28] Whether such a view conforms to reality is an issue on which scholars violently disagree—at the level of philosophical speculation. But even the most deterministic systems theorists may exhibit a strong policy orientation, apparently reflecting a conviction that the system is not deterministic so far as their own relations to it are concerned.

What may be gained by viewing the state, the interna-

[28] Commenting on this issue, J. D. Singer has observed that the tendency is "to move, in a system-oriented model, away from notions implying much national autonomy and independence of choice toward a more deterministic orientation." "The Level of Analysis Problem in International Relations," in *World Politics*, 1961, v. 14, p. 81. For an example of this tendency, see the exercise in building a model international system, by A. L. Burns: "From Balance to Deterrence," in *World Politics*, 1957, v. 9, pp. 494*ff*. In introducing this model, Burns posits a "strongly deterministic role of military technology in current international affairs," and explicitly rejects the relevance of the sciences of human behavior—psychology, sociology, and anthropology—for the analysis of international political systems.

tional system, or any other social system as a self-regulating set of patterns is debatable. At the very least, those
who explicitly or implicitly attribute autonomic properties
to social systems should take care to state precisely *in
what sense* they conceive the operation of the system to
be determined by forces beyond the control of its human
components.

This issue poses the distinction (noted early in this
chapter) between two different concepts of determinism:
the first, conceived in terms of absolute, 100 per cent
predictability, and hence for practical purposes a denial
of volition; the second, conceived in terms of strong probability of occurrence of a class of events based on considerable (though not necessarily total) statistical regularity in a large aggregate of cases.

It is difficult to locate convincing exhibits of the first.
Pure 100 per cent determinism seems to be largely a
hypothetical man-of-straw, set up for forensic purposes
largely in order to shoot it down. None of the so-called
impressionistic determinists have denied human capacity
to make ineffective choices, ineffective in the sense that
environing conditions constitute barriers to desired accomplishment. As noted above, and as we shall emphasize
again in the next chapter, impressionistic determinists
nearly always leave open a line for semantic retreat.

Statistical determinism, conceived in terms of average
behavior in large aggregates of cases, seems to be something quite different. This is the character of demographic
projections, market predictions, actuarial rate-tables, and
the like. It is essentially the character of the Stewart-
Warntz "law" of potential of population (noted previously
on page 46).

Critics have attacked the Stewart-Warntz "law" on various grounds. In particular they have stressed its deter-

ministic overtones.[29] The Stewart-Warntz "law" is deterministic *only* in the sense that behavior is predicted without reference to the volition of particular individuals in the aggregate under consideration. The analyst may, and usually does, anticipate deviations from the average. He may regard such deviations as inconsequential for the problem in hand. Or he may build them into his prediction, as anticipated margin of error.

Here one confronts another exhibit of semantic confusion. Most of those accustomed to using such methods in social analysis would stoutly deny that their statistical operations carry any philosophical overtones regarding human freedom to choose among alternatives. But humanists, and many historians, geographers, and political scientists, *unaccustomed to quantitative methods, and acutely attuned to deterministic overtones on any wavelength,* seem to be quite prone to construing statistical correlations as a subtle, even sinister, device to bootleg philosophical determinism in through the rear door.[30]

Terminology susceptible of deterministic interpretation in systemic theories of international politics may well reflect in some degree the intellectual mores of the mathematicians, physical scientists, and economists who have lately invaded this field in some force. But wholly aside from the philosophical implications which less quantitatively oriented scholars are likely to read into these inno-

[29] See, for example, O. H. K. Spate, "Quantity and Quality in Geography," in *Annals,* Association of American Geographers, 1960, v. 50, pp. 377, 390.

[30] This issue turns largely, it would appear, on the range of connotations which different specialists read into the terms "law," "cause," and the like. These terms may stand for quite different concepts in science and in moral philosophy, for example. For discussions of this problem, see Emrys Jones, "Cause and Effect in Human Geography," in *Annals,* Association of American Geographers, 1956, v. 46, pp. 369ff, and T. D. Weldon, *The Vocabulary of Politics,* Penguin, 1953, pp. 61ff.

vations, there seems to be a question whether the aggregates of units in any international system are large enough, and whether these units exhibit sufficient homogeneity, to render tenable even a purely statistical type of determinism in international political analysis.

In this connection, it may be noted in passing that a tentative attempt to use the Stewart-Warntz population-distance formula to plot the geographic "field" of political influence or attraction (that is, the political potential) of the major units of the society of nations produced a cartogram radically incongruent with international patterns repeatedly confirmed by "common-sense" observation. This led Stewart to conclude that "weighting factors" would have to be introduced where the social units comprising the system exhibit wide variations in levels of technology or in other essential respects. One weighting factor tried out was "social mass," defined as the "tonnage of material" per capita per year, which has been "moved or fabricated for social purposes" in the political communities compared. This helped to bring the population-distance formula into closer congruence with impressionistic conclusions.

Whether these experiments yielded much new knowledge about political relations is certainly debatable. But they did put the problem of describing international patterns into fresh perspective. They evoked queries as to the relative significance of different environmental factors in estimating the political capabilities of nations. At the very least, Stewart's sortie from physics into international politics provided an example of new insights derived in the process of disconfirming a propounded hypothesis.[31]

[31] For a brief account of Stewart's sortie into political science, see his "Natural Law Factors in United States Foreign Policy," in *Social Science*, 1954, v. 29, pp. 127ff. The title of this article is misleading: "natural" laws in Stewart's idiom meaning the laws of physics.

ENVIRONMENTAL DETERMINISM

It remains to deal briefly with the environmental neo-determinism that has attracted some notice in recent years. We refer especially to the work of the Australian geographer Griffith Taylor and the British geographer O. H. K. Spate, who went to the Australian National University in the early 1950's. Taylor openly asserted that he was an environmental determinist: sometimes he called himself a "stop-and-go" determinist, sometimes a "scientific" determinist. His thesis is essentially that knowledge of the non-human environment enables one to predict what will and will not be attempted in a given locality, as well as what can be accomplished. With reference to places like Antarctica, or the arid interior of Australia, he claimed that "it is absurd to say that man can choose which he pleases among many possible directions." [32]

Spate takes a similar line, but stresses more explicitly the implications of accumulated knowledge and habituation. People learn, often the hard way, what can and what cannot be accomplished in a given milieu. They also become habituated to accepting the limits of what, in their society, is believed to be possible. Always, he says, "we choose in a context determined by our previous choices, and so backwards to the initial act of our conception, which was certainly not our choice—and perhaps not even a choice at all." [33]

In the end, Taylor (implicitly) and Spate (rather more explicitly) arrive at a philosophical posture that seems to

[32] Griffith Taylor et al., Geography in the Twentieth Century, Philosophical Library, 1951, pp. 11, 15.
[33] O. H. K. Spate, "How Determined Is Possibilism?" in Geographical Studies, 1957, v. 4, pp. 3, 7. Compare the view of the American geographer S. B. Jones: "The environment does not determine, is not truly an active influence, but offers possibilities to man, from which he chooses. His choices, to be sure, are not unlimited and not actually free, since they are conditioned by both nature and his own culture." "Geographical Thought in the United States," in Perspective, Summer, 1955, pp. 59, 76.

us to approximate a probabilistic behavioralism based on statistical averages. They use the rhetoric to which earlier impressionistic determinists were addicted. But their discourse, especially Spate's, also suggests the kind of probabilistic reasoning that underlies statistical determinism.[84]

This brings us to the point where we shall leave the issue of environmental determinism for the moment: namely, the thesis that assumption of a philosophical posture of determinism may profoundly affect the nuances of one's thinking about man-milieu relationships, but that most deterministic statements can be translated into probabilistic sentences, and that these latter generally come closer to the philosophical posture that seems to characterize most people's image of such relationships, at least in technologically advanced societies.

[84] Spate specifically recommends thinking of human choices in terms of a "balance of probabilities," and then concludes: "I think that this would go far to bridge the gap; though in the last resort there will always be the stubborn divergence between those who believe that man is broadly a free agent, and those who believe that his ends and means are chosen for him by God or chance or chemistry." *Op. cit.*, p. 11.

4

FREE-WILL ENVIRONMENTALISM

WE NOTED in the preceding chapter how rarely a posture
of strict determinism is maintained, and how frequently
deterministic verbs are qualified by words asserting or implying some freedom of choice among alternatives. This
well-known method of eating one's cake and having it,
too, constitutes a sufficiently distinctive attitude towards
man-milieu relationships to merit some further consideration. This posture is variously called mild environmentalism, physical environmentalism, or simply environmentalism. A more apt label would be free-will environmentalism.

Those who speak in this idiom populate their universe
with "influences," derived in the main from the nonhuman environment, sometimes called simply "geography"
or "nature." But they avoid verbs that might cast doubt
on volition. In this watered-down derivative of environmental determinism, man is assumed to have a free will.
Nature gives him instructions, but he is capable of choosing, however unwisely, to disregard them. Even Semple
(whose addiction to deterministic rhetoric was noted in
the preceding chapter) explicitly disavowed a strict deterministic posture. She preferred, she said, to speak of "geographic factors and influences," rather than "geographic
control," and to avoid altogether the notion of geographic
"determinants." [1]

[1] E. C. Semple, *Influences of Geographic Environment*, Holt,
1911, p. vii. It is impossible to decide from either the vocabulary
used or the context whether Semple was really a confirmed determinist in a philosophical sense. See J. K. Wright's discussion of this
issue in "Miss Semple's 'Influences of Geographic Environment,'"
in *Geographical Review*, 1962, v. 52, pp. 346ff.

FREE-WILL ENVIRONMENTALISM

The rhetoric of environmental "influences" clearly embraces a range of philosophical postures. At one extreme, it merges into determinism. At the other, such rhetoric, often rich in teleological imagery, may be simply a semantic device to obtain dramatic literary effects. Often it is quite impossible to decide, either from the words used or from the context in which they are used, exactly what posture towards environmental relationships the speaker desires to convey. A few examples will illustrate this uncertainty.

First, the opening sentences of Semple's master work, *Influences of Geographic Environment:* "Man is a product of the earth's surface. . . . The earth has *mothered* him, *fed* him, *set* him tasks, *directed* his thoughts, *confronted* him with difficulties that have strengthened his body and sharpened his wits, *given* him his problems . . . and at the same time *whispered* hints for their solution" (italics added).[2]

Next, a passage from a highly regarded book by a recognized authority on Japanese history: "The mountains of Japan have *pushed* the Japanese out upon the seas. . . . Sea routes have *beckoned* the Japanese. . . . The factor of geographic isolation during the past two thousand years *has helped fashion* national traits which eventually, and *almost inevitably, led* Japan to political isolation and to crushing defeat in war" (italics added).[3]

Now, a passage from a work on Russian national character: ". . . when we think of Russia we must evoke the image of the mighty plain and its exacting climate, which have *dominated* and *conditioned* the lives of the Russian people for countless generations, and will continue to *dominate* them until man succeeds in shutting

[2] Semple, *op. cit.*, p. 1.
[3] E. O. Reischauer, *Japan: Past and Present*, Knopf, 1946, pp. 5, 8.

out the sky. The plain is a *positive influence*. It has certain characteristics which are faithfully reflected in the make-up of its inhabitants. I do not say that aspect for aspect the people have been molded in the image of the plain, but I do say that certain characteristics of the Russian temperament . . . have been *brought out* and *magnified* by their physical environment, which has therefore *helped to make them* what they are" (italics added).[4]

Fourth, a characterization of the Chinese landscape from the pen of the late G. B. Cressey: It is "a biophysical unity, knit together as intimately as a tree and the soil from which it grows. So deeply is man rooted in the earth that there is but one all-inclusive unity—not man and nature as separate phenomena but a *single organic whole*" (italics added).[5]

Fifth, some excerpts from an article by the late N. J. Spykman who, perhaps more than any other modern political scientist, emphasized the international political significance of location, distance, space, and areal distributions and configurations: "Size *affects* the relative strength of a state in the struggle for power. Natural resources *influence* population density and economic structure, which in themselves are factors in the formulation of policy. . . . Topography affects strength *because of its influence* on unity and internal coherence. Climate, *affecting* transportation and setting limits to the possibility of agricultural production, *conditions* the economic structure of the state, and thus, indirectly but unmistakably, foreign policy. . . . On the establishment of a communication system, which is in turn one of the most effective means

[4] Edward Crankshaw, *Russia and the Russians*, Viking, 1948, pp. 19-20.
[5] G. B. Cressey, *Asia's Lands and Peoples*, McGraw-Hill, 1944, p. 35.

of counteracting separatist tendencies, the shape and topography of a state have a *direct influence*. . . . States
that are long and narrow in shape . . . *tend inevitably*
to disintegrate. . . . Mountain distribution, the *chief
cause* of the present ethnic distribution, has *exercised* on
Switzerland a definitely *decentralizing effect*. . . . In
Siberia, climate *adds* its decentralizing *influence* to that
of topography. . . . Because the cataracts on the Dnieper
below Kiev formed a barrier to communication, Kiev gave
way to Moscow as the seat of the government, which
from its position on the Moscova . . . can extend its
centralizing *influence* to all the corners of European Russia. A similar network of rivers converging on Paris *makes*
that city the *inevitable* center of France and *centers*
France *inevitably* about Paris" (italics added).[6]

One could extend this exhibit of environmentalistic
rhetoric, but a few more brief examples will have to suffice.

"The *influence* of geography on history is a common-
place of modern thought" (italics added).[7]

"The general character of England's foreign policy is
determined by the *immutable conditions* of her *geographical situation* . . . " (italics added).[8]

"*Nature itself had made* Francis I, who reigned in Paris,
his [Charles V's] rival and his enemy" (italics added).[9]

[6] N. J. Spykman, "Geography and Foreign Policy," in *American
Political Science Review*, 1938, v. 32, pp. 28, 30-36.

[7] Sir Austen Chamberlain, "The Permanent Bases of British Foreign Policy," in *Foreign Affairs*, 1931, v. 9, p. 538.

[8] Eyre Crowe, "Memorandum on the Present State of British
Relations with France and Germany," British Foreign Office, Jan-
uary 1, 1907; reprinted in *British Documents on the Origins of the
War*, edited by G. P. Gooch and H. Temperley, H. M. Stationery
Office, London, 1928, v. 3, p. 402.

[9] Jules Cambon, "The Permanent Bases of French Foreign Policy," in *Foreign Affairs Reader*, edited by H. F. Armstrong, Harper,
1947, p. 109.

FREE-WILL ENVIRONMENTALISM

"*Location tends to make* a state a land power or a sea power . . . " (italics added).[10]

Griffith Taylor (whose self-styled "scientific determinism" was noted in the preceding chapter) speaks repeatedly of "Nature's master plan for the world." Man, in his idiom, is merely the "agent" who reads Nature's blueprint and succeeds or fails in proportion as he follows the instructions.[11]

Erich Zimmermann, in a standard treatise on resources and industries, goes still further. Nature, he says, "does infinitely more than merely set the outer limits within which human arts and wants can operate. *She makes suggestions* and man is wise enough to listen. At times . . . *she lures* him by rich rewards or *blocks his road* with discouraging *threats*" (italics added).[12]

Spykman voiced the same thought when he insisted: "*Geography* does not determine, but it does condition; it not only offers possibilities for use, *it demands* that they be used; man's only freedom lies in his capacity to use well or ill or to modify for better or for worse those possibilities" (italics added).[18]

How is one to construe the teleological environmentalistic imagery that recurs so frequently in discussions of human affairs? Manifestly, not literally! Mountains do not "push"; seas do not "beckon"; geography does not "demand"; insularity does not lead "inevitably" to anything or anywhere.

One possible hypothesis, of course, is that speakers who indulge in such rhetoric are indeed naïve believers in a

[10] N. D. Palmer and H. C. Perkins, *International Relations*, Houghton-Mifflin, 1953, p. 78.
[11] Griffith Taylor *et al.*, *Geography in the Twentieth Century*, Philosophical Library, 1951, pp. 14, 16, 161.
[12] Erich Zimmermann, *World Resources and Industries*, Harper, revised edition, 1951, p. 11.
[18] Spykman, "Geography and Foreign Policy," p. 30n.

nonhuman environment endowed with animistic, human-like behavioral characters. Read in context, however, even the most extreme teleological statements rarely appear to justify the conclusion that the author intended to ascribe human-like purposes and actions to the nonhuman environment.

Another possible hypothesis is that environmentalistic rhetoric is simply a sort of fanciful poetic license. Shelley began a famous poem about a skylark with the familiar lines:

> "Hail to thee, blithe spirit!
> Bird thou never wert."

Judged by standard lexical canons, this statement is patently contrary to fact. In everyday speech and in every known dictionary definition, a skylark is a bird, whether Shelley says so or not. But in the context of the poem, the quoted lines are not confusing. For the poet, words are like colors in a painting, or sounds of different pitch and timbre in music. Using words to evoke moods and images, regardless of accepted lexical meanings, is inherent in the art of poesy, and is appropriately called poetic license.

Poetic license is not confined to poetry. It has invaded fields in which lexical precision is of the essence of communication. Writers who purport to speak scientifically, or at least precisely, about human behavior and relationships may also play fast-and-loose with the verbal language, as we have seen in some of the examples quoted above.

Such rhetoric is a fanciful and imprecise mode of expression. We have heard it defended, by editors and publishers as well as by authors of serious works of scholarship. They assert, among other things, that poetic license infuses prose with a sense of struggle and drama, and is necessary in order to capture readers and hold their attention—and to sell books, no doubt! Be that as it may, poetic license in any context of man-milieu relationship is likely to foster teleological imagery at the very least, and in addition to constitute an obstacle to precise description and explanation.

There is, however, at least one other way to interpret environmentalistic rhetoric. Quite often, it would appear, authors employ action-verbs with an environmental factor or set of factors as the grammatical subject, but in a sense neither teleological nor poetic.

Take the verb *influence,* for example. This is probably the most overworked verb in the environmentalist vocabulary. The essence of dictionary definitions of influence is: some activity on the part of a person or thing that produces without apparent force an effect on another person or thing. The father speaks and thereby influences his child. The traffic officer blows his whistle and thereby influences the motorist. Then, by a sort of analogical extension, an author speaks of geographic location or climate or a new machine or some other nonhuman factor influencing people to do so-and-so.

Construed in context, such seemingly teleological statements appear frequently to be a sort of verbal shorthand, to connote that the "influenced" person perceived the environmental factor in question; that he evaluated it with reference to his purposes; and that he acted in the light of the conclusions reached.

This was the sense in which we construed the passage in the textbook on seapower (quoted in the preceding chapter). In reviewing that book we said: ". . . neither 'sparse resources' nor any other environmental condition ever *drove* England to do anything, and *geography* did not *destine* England to command the seas. We interpret the passage to mean simply that available resources ashore, configuration of lands and seas, and other conditions latent in the environment enabled Englishmen to achieve the kind of history which they did in fact make for themselves." [14]

One could similarly construe the whole battery of action-verbs when employed with environmental subjects. In such usage, the force of the verb—ranging from determine, or control, to influence—may be construed merely as expressing the speaker's estimate of the odds that the environed individual or group would recognize and heed the limitations latent in the milieu in question. Thus, when one reads in the book on Japan (quoted above) that "sea routes beckoned the Japanese abroad," perhaps all that the author intended to communicate is that, at a certain stage in Japanese history, substantial numbers of Japanese people envisaged more attractive opportunities in seafaring than in farming or in other occupations ashore. A very similar passage occurs in Semple's work, previously cited. With reference to colonial New England, she said: "While the sea drew, the land drove in the same direction." [15]

Now, compare Semple's rhetoric with the following passage from W. C. Putnam's textbook of geology: "The lavish supply of boulders on the farms of New England was a source . . . of . . . backbreaking toil. So much labor was involved in clearing fields . . . that more than one young man was readily convinced that a life at sea could be no harder. . . ." [16] This passage, we think, should refute the argument that teleological imagery is a requisite of vivid prose. Clearly implicit in Putnam's statement is the thesis that the milieu "influences" human

[14] Review by H. Sprout, of E. B. Potter *et al.*, *The United States and World Sea Power*, Prentice-Hall, 1955; reviewed in *United States Naval Institute Proceedings*, February, 1956, v. 82, p. 213.

[15] *Influences of Geographic Environment*, p. 15.

[16] W. C. Putnam, *Geology*, Oxford University Press, 1964, p. 319.

choices and decisions only via perception and other psychological processes, a thesis to which we shall return in
Chapters VI and VII.

To interpret teleological imagery as merely a sort of
verbal shorthand, and nothing more, probably oversim-
plifies what is manifestly a tangled state of affairs. Close
study of texts seems to us to confirm daily observation
that there is some latent disposition in nearly everyone
to think as well as to speak in teleological metaphors.
There is probably much truth in the assertions of environmental theorists, geographers in particular, that environmentalistic rhetoric predisposes as well as reflects a
propensity to "pre-select" and ascribe "causal" property
to such phenomena as the layout of lands and seas, landscape configurations, soil and mineral distributions, climatic patterns, and the like. By such pre-selection, the
critics have contended, one closes his mind to the possible
relevance and significance of other factors. Research thus
becomes a search for correlations between pre-selected
causes and the events to be explained or predicted.[17]

This line of criticism seems generally to be well
founded. Anyone who has read in the literature of geography, history, and the social sciences will recall examples
of apparent reasoning from pre-selected environmental
"causes." But when critics of such practice stress the importance of approaching problems with an "open mind,"
they had better be sure that they do not mean an empty

[17] For representative exhibits of this line of criticism, see
K. G. T. Clark, "Certain Underpinnings of Our Arguments in
Human Geography," in *Transactions and Papers*, Institute of Brit-
ish Geographers, 1950, No. 16, pp. 15, 19; C. O. Sauer, "Recent
Developments in Cultural Geography," in *Recent Developments in
the Social Sciences*, edited by E. C. Hayes, Lippincott, 1927, p. 175;
Richard Hartshorne, *The Nature of Geography*, Association of
American Geographers, 1939, pp. 120*ff*; T. C. Platt, "Environ-
mentalism vs. Geography," in *American Journal of Sociology*,
1948, v. 53, pp. 351*ff*.

mind, or even a completely unprejudiced mind. No one ever approaches any problem with an empty mind, and rarely without predispositions. One always starts with some hypothesis, perhaps no more than a vague hunch, but an hypothesis nonetheless as to what factors are relevant and significant. Otherwise he could not even define a problem for study. One's initial hypothesis inescapably predisposes him more or less toward certain data and interpretations in preference to others. The crucial issue is whether he is capable of modifying his initial hypothesis as more and different kinds of data are brought to his attention.

Criticism of any explanatory procedure solely on the ground that it predisposes one to regard certain factors as more important than others, indicates misconception of the nature of all scientific analysis. But there is certainly justification for criticizing anyone for dogmatically refusing to examine alternative hypotheses and data. Such a person has truly built for himself a conceptual jail from which to contemplate the universe. It is to the propensity of certain students of human affairs to do just that, rather than their alleged predisposition towards certain "causal" factors, that the critics of environmentalism should direct their fire.

The battle over environmentalism was fought, and won at least in principle, a generation ago within the discipline of geography. No geographer known to us would today endorse the environmentalistic rhetoric that still clutters the literature of politics, especially international politics. In recent years, geographic theorists have repeatedly asserted that environmentalism is a dead issue no longer worth debating.[18]

Whether the environmentalist posture is worth further

[18] On this issue, see in particular Richard Hartshorne, *Perspective on the Nature of Geography*, Rand-McNally, 1959, pp. 55ff.

examination depends, in part, on the audience to which one is speaking. The mistaken idea that geographers are primarily concerned with the influence of the natural environment on human activities is still very much alive among non-geographers, especially among political scientists. Writers on political subjects continue to indulge in environmental rhetoric and teleological imagery when discussing the political significance of geographic location, distance, space, distribution, and configuration. Influential political theorists who have given specific attention to the bearings of geography on politics have identified geography with physical environmentalism. This identification is implicit in the writings of Spykman (quoted above). It is explicit in the discussion of political geography in Quincy Wright's treatise on *The Study of International Relations*. Probably no single work has served so many teachers of international politics as a guide to the interdisciplinary ramifications of their subject.

Wright characterizes political geography in a manner which every geographic theorist known to us would reject *in toto*. "As an aspect of international relations," Wright says, political geography is the "science of relating the physical environment to world politics, and the art, sometimes called *Geopolitik*, of utilizing the physical environment in world politics." He recognizes different schools of geographic thought; but he seems to believe that political geography in its international aspect is concerned mainly with establishing the "influence" of nonhuman factors of environment on the structure, power, and foreign policies of states. He speaks almost, though not quite exclusively, in the vocabulary of environmentalism. For example, within the space of five pages he employs the word *influence* not less than twenty times, with no explanation as to what he means by it. He also uses such expressions as "the environment demands . . ."; "to think geographi-

FREE-WILL ENVIRONMENTALISM

cally" is to be alert to environmental influences . . .";
and more of the same.[19]

As previously noted, geographic theorists have been to
great pains in recent years to dissociate their discipline
from a teleological environmentalist posture. But it seems
likely that more contemporary students of politics have
derived their ideas of what political geography is about
from Spykman and Wright than from professional geographers. We have read many pages and listened to much
talk about the "influence" of location, distance, space,
layout of lands and seas, land-surface configuration, distribution of material resources, climate and other earth
phenomena, on the policies and political relations of states.
But the meaning of "influence" is almost never made explicit. Those who attribute "influence" to factors of the
nonhuman environment are rarely prepared, it would
seem, to describe at all precisely the mechanisms and
processes by which such "influences" either become operative in the decisions of statesmen or in the states of
affairs that result from their undertakings.

In spite of all that has been said in the foregoing pages,
we anticipate that many readers (though probably not
many geographers) will still query what harm results
from environmentalistic figures of speech. We hear them
asking: Do you mean to say that environmental factors
do *not* "influence" people's choice and decisions and accomplishments? Our answer, as already intimated, turns
on what one means by "influence," an issue which we
hope to resolve satisfactorily in Chapters VI and VII.

[19] Quincy Wright, *The Study of International Relations*, Appleton-Century-Crofts, 1955, ch. 24. The above paragraph stands
pretty much as it appeared in the earlier version of our discussion
of man-milieu relationship hypotheses. A fresh reading of Wright's
chapter on "political geography" confirms our conclusion that this
widely read book instructs non-geographers, in effect, that geography and physical environmentalism are one and the same subject.

5

POSSIBILISM

THE DOCTRINE called environmental possibilism, or simply possibilism, represents an historic reversal of perspective towards man-milieu relationships. In contrast to environmental determinism, and its watered-down derivative, free-will environmentalism, the central tenet of possibilism is that the initiative lies with man, not with the milieu which encompasses him. Possibilism rejects the idea of controls, or influences, pressing man along a road set by Nature or any other environing conditions. The milieu, in the possibilist doctrine, does not compel or direct man to do anything. The milieu is simply there—clay, sometimes malleable, sometimes refractory, but clay nonetheless at the disposal of man the builder.

In the possibilist doctrine, the milieu is conceived as a set of opportunities and limitations. With respect to any *given* project, decision, undertaking, or course of action, a possibilistic analysis directs attention to those factors of the milieu that may affect the operational result, outcome, performance, or accomplishment. In the formative stage of the doctrine, opportunities generally were stressed more than limitations. This emphasis was given classic expression in the often quoted words of the French geographer Lucien Febvre:

"Des nécessités, nulle part. Des possibilités, partout. Et l'homme, maître des possibilités, juge de leur emploi: c'est le placer dès lors au premier plan par un renversement nécessaire: l'homme et non plus la terre, ni les influences du climat ni les conditions determinantes des lieux." [1]

[1] Lucien Febvre, *La terre et l'évolution humaine*, Paris, 1922, p. 284; published in English translation, by Knopf, 1925, entitled: *A Geographical Introduction to History*.

This thesis evolved within at least two different contexts: in Europe (later in America) as a reaction among geographers against the doctrine of environmental determinism; in America, as a philosophical revolt against the deterministic evolutionism of Herbert Spencer.[2]

The geographic origin of possibilism has been attributed to the "French school" of geography in general, and to Videl de la Blache in particular. It has been suggested that possibilism was especially attractive to Frenchmen around the turn of the century when German geographers seemed to be building a geopolitical case for further "inevitable" expansion of the German Empire.[3]

Concurrently, in America the central tenet of possibilism was gaining expression in the philosophical doctrine of pragmatism. During the middle decades of the nineteenth century, the British philosopher Herbert Spencer had extended Darwin's evolutionary hypothesis into a social doctrine of extreme conservatism. Only the fittest could survive in society as in Nature; and for Spencer, worldly success was the test of fitness. The poor and underprivileged were by definition unfit. Government-sponsored reforms were socially injurious, since they tended to prolong the lives of the unfit. In the long run, such policies were also fruitless, since they represented attempts to thwart the inexorable law of nature.

The philosophical doctrine of pragmatism, associated in particular with the names of William James and John Dewey, represented an intellectual revolt against what

[2] In general, see George Tatham, "Environmentalism and Possibilism," in *Geography in the Twentieth Century*, edited by Griffith Taylor, Philosophical Library, 1951, pp. 128*ff;* Richard Hartshorne, *Perspective on the Nature of Geography*, Rand-McNally, 1959, pp. 56*ff;* and Richard Hofstadter, *Social Darwinism in American Thought*, revised edition, Beacon Press, 1955, ch. 7.

[3] Tatham, *op. cit.*, pp. 151*ff;* also O. H. K. Spate, "How Determined Is Possibilism?" in *Geographical Studies*, 1957, v. 4, pp. 3, 8.

Richard Hofstadter calls "the cold determinism of Spencer's philosophy." Pragmatism also reflected the American belief in progress. Hofstadter continues: "Pragmatism was absorbed into the national culture when men were thinking of manipulation and control. Spencerianism had been the philosophy of inevitability; pragmatism became the philosophy of possibility. . . . Spencer had been content to assume the environment as a fixed norm. . . . Pragmatism, entertaining a more positive view of the activities of the organism, looked upon the environment as something that could be manipulated. . . . As Spencer had stood for . . . control of man by the environment, the pragmatists stood for freedom and control of the environment by man." In the instrumental thinking of Dewey, the function of "knowledge" became "not mere passive adjustment but the manipulation of the environment to provide 'consummatory' satisfactions." [4]

The older determinism and environmentalism embodied the idea that the human species, like subhuman species, could survive only through successful adaptation to a milieu largely beyond human capacity to control. In contrast, environmental possibilism, especially in America, radiated a belief in man's almost limitless ability to mold and modify Nature to his own purposes. "Most men [observed the American geographer Isaiah Bowman] take the view that the world is their oyster. They are out for conquest." [5]

This "conquest" took various forms and proceeded at different rates from one country to another. But in all the more technically advanced societies, man, the new "geographic agent," was transforming the face of the earth. Frequently the social results were disastrous, or

[4] Hofstadter, *op. cit.*, pp. 104, 123, 124, 125, 136 and *passim*.
[5] Isaiah Bowman, *Geography in Relation to the Social Sciences*, Scribner, 1934, p. 7.

potentially disastrous, as well as beneficent. As far back as the 1860's, the alarm was sounded by George Perkins Marsh, an extraordinarily gifted American scholar, diplomat, lawyer, and politician. His pioneering book, *The Earth as Modified by Human Action,*[6] was followed over the years by a burgeoning literature that described and decried the reckless denudation of the earth, progressive pollution of water, air, and food supplies, urban crowding and traffic congestion, and other consequences of the still accelerating technological revolution.[7]

Though manipulation, modification, and control of the milieu are the predominant themes in much of the literature written in the possibilist vein, even the most optimistic possibilists came in due course to recognize that every milieu presents limitations as well as opportunities. What is possible in an instrumental sense to achieve varies with changes in technology. Every mechanical invention, every improved tool, every new skill, alters and generally (though not always) increases someone's ability to make his purposes prevail over nature and against the resistance of his fellow men. Obstacles—for example, prairie sod—that are insurmountable with one set of tools yield to another. The relation between technology and instrumental ability to achieve given objectives is too well understood to require extended demonstration.

Though nearly always important, and sometimes strategic, instrumental limitations are by no means the only ones, or necessarily the most significant. A point often

[6] Originally published in 1863, as *Man and Nature,* Marsh's book was revised and retitled *The Earth as Modified by Human Action,* Scribner, 1874.

[7] Many of the ramifications of this process are described in the symposium, *Man's Role in Changing the Face of the Earth,* edited by W. L. Thomas, Jr., University of Chicago Press, 1956. See, in particular, the paper by C. L. Glacken, "Changing Ideas of the Habitable World," *ibid.,* pp. 70ff.

ignored, or at least minimized, is the factor of cost in general, and in particular the comparative costs of alternative undertakings both of which are technically feasible. In the words of the Canadian geographer, George Tatham: "the opportunities offered by any environment are not all equal. Some demand little effort from man, others continued struggle; some yield large, others meager returns. The ratio between effort and return can be looked upon as the price. . . ."[8]

Bowman put the same idea in his often quoted "punch line": Men "cannot move mountains without floating a bond issue." And he added: Mankind "conforms to many defective layouts because it would cost too much to alter them. . . . The mind of man . . . remembers events, facts, and relationships, and actively experiments, observes, and generalizes to see how and why things work or can be made to work. This looks as if there were only the broadest bounds to man's spread and his power to use the earth. Time has taught him, however, that there is a higher law than that of making things work in spite of or against natural limitations. He can build a comfortable well-lighted city and provide education, opera, and games at the South Pole. . . . But will it pay?"[9]

A corollary of this possibilist concept of cost is another proposition, one that becomes increasingly relevant with every passing year: that the problem of overcoming limitations of the nonhuman environment becomes ever more economic, political, and broadly social, rather than narrowly technological. This is conspicuously the case in the more advanced industrial societies. In those societies there is sufficient available scientific and engineering knowledge,

[8] Tatham, "Environmentalism and Possibilism," in *Geography in the Twentieth Century,* 1st edition, p. 160.
[9] Bowman, *Geography in Relation to the Social Sciences,* pp. 3, 4, 164.

and sufficient equipment and human skills, to accomplish a great deal more than is ever undertaken. More railroads could be modernized. More and better highways could be built. More airways could be extended and improved. More ores could be mined and refined, and more synthetic substitutes for scarce materials could be produced. More people could be more adequately fed and clothed. More and better medical services could be furnished. Better schools and universities could be provided for more children and youth. More buildings could be cooled in hot damp climates. Sea water could be de-salted and more arid acres irrigated. Exploration of outer space could be accelerated. Weapons could be further improved. Industries could be relocated to make them less vulnerable to airborne attacks. The list of *technically* feasible projects is long, and grows longer year by year.

When new projects are contemplated, at least in the technically more advanced societies, the issue is rarely one of technical feasibility alone. The controlling factors are often not technical feasibility at all, but rather such considerations as: How much will the undertaking cost? Who is going to pay? Which projects should have priority?

Before the industrial era, shortage of equipment and skills set severe limits to human ability to cope with heat, cold, dampness, aridity, distance, terrain, deeply buried minerals, predatory animals, bacteria and viruses, and other nonhuman obstacles. Such limitations still prevail in many of the underdeveloped countries today. But technological advances have progressively widened and extended human capacity to cope with the nonhuman environment.

At the higher levels of technological knowledge and economic development, limitations on what can be accomplished tend to shift to other sectors of the milieu. In particular, limitations imposed by the social order—institutions, values, role allocations, and the like—tend to become progressively more important than limitations imposed by the state of technology or the availability of natural resources.

This is not an argument for the thesis that either technology or the social order can erase differentials between societies arising from differences in their respective nonhuman environments. It is manifestly true that many more units of energy are required to heat buildings in winter and to keep them tolerably cool in summer in the savage midcontinental climate of North America than in the milder climates of Western Europe. It is likewise true that greater expenditures of energy are required to haul ores and other heavy freight across the vast continental space of the Soviet Union than are required to perform similar tasks in a small country such as Britain.

Every country has so-called "natural" advantages and disadvantages in comparison with any other one. Technological advances may narrow these differences, provided certain social conditions prevail. In any case, one consequence of achieving a higher level of productivity per capita is to enable a people to pay a higher price for overcoming "natural" obstacles which, at a lower technological and economic level, might be insurmountable. The more efficient a society's equipment, and the greater and more diverse the knowledge and skills of its members, the greater becomes their capacity to master the limitations of their nonhuman environment—and to do so at a price compatible with their idea of a tolerable standard of living.

An important, and frequently overlooked, aspect of nearly all discussions of environmental opportunities and limitations is the significance of differential variation through time among different sets of environing factors.

Take, for example, limitations on human achievement implicit in the physical earth. Such limitations vary through time, in part because of changes in the earth's physical structure, in part because of other events which widen or restrict the range of effective human choice.

Some of the changes in the earth's structure result from physical processes of nature: earth slipping, volcanoes erupting, rocks falling, water flowing and freezing, wind blowing, plants, animals and micro-organisms proliferating, etc. Sometimes these natural processes cause human catastrophes: earthquakes, floods, famines, epidemics, and the like.

Alongside these natural phenomena are changes in the earth wrought by the hand of man. With advancing knowledge, and more efficient tools and skills, men have produced ever greater changes in the physical structure of the earth. They have dug canals and changed the course of rivers. They have built harbors and tunneled through mountains. They have cut down forests and planted new ones. They have depleted the soil and sometimes restored its fertility. They have made deserts bloom and have turned verdant landscapes into deserts. They have pumped oil and water from underground reservoirs, moved bodies of soil and rock, and used up irreplaceable minerals. They have smashed atoms and fused them, creating new elements and transmuting matter into energy. In these and in many other ways, men have altered the physical structure of their habitat. Such basic structural changes have affected in varying degrees the capabilities and relations of individuals, groups, and nations.

A good example, from international politics, is the building of the Suez Canal, opened in 1869. That engineering feat created a shipway across the narrow isthmus which separates the Mediterranean Sea from the Red Sea and Indian Ocean. The canal cut several thousand miles from sea voyages between European ports and southern and eastern Asia. It soon became one of the most heavily used waterways of international commerce. But the canal also became the strategic backbone of the British Empire. This led within a few years to British occupation of Egypt and military domination of the canal. The existence of the canal also affected Britain's political relations with every country fronting on the Mediterranean; it tightened Britain's military grip on the Indian Ocean; and in subtle ways it also affected political capabilities and relationships in more distant parts of the earth.

As another example, consider the international implications of the heavy and progressive depletion of North American forests, soils, mineral fuels, and other natural resources. This depletion has been going on for well over a century. The rate of depletion has accelerated sharply in recent decades. Consumption reached a peak during World War II. It is climbing to still higher peaks in our time. These alterations of the physical geography of North America have various political implications. Not the least of them is the increasing dependence of the United States on imported iron ore and other basic raw materials in a period of continuing uncertainty in the political relations of all states and regions.

The social consequences of man-made changes in the earth's surface and subsurface have been great in the past and seem likely to be even greater in the future. But great as such changes have been, they are overshadowed in their social effects by other changes—especially advances in science and engineering—which, while not actually altering the earth's physical structure substantially, have given new meanings and new values to such geographic dimensions as location, distance, space, the configuration of lands and seas, and the distributions of climate and natural resources.

Consider, for example, the changes that have taken place in the military properties of oceanic space during the past sixty or seventy years. Theories of seapower which appeared, as late as 1900, to be as permanent as the oceans themselves have become progressively obsolescent. The oceans and seas (one set of environmental factors) have remained approximately constant in terms of this particular problem. Their size and shape have not changed significantly. But the activities which men can carry out upon the oceans and seas have changed profoundly. Ships have been designed to cruise greater distances without refueling. Methods for refueling at sea have been perfected. Submarines have become formidable weapons with which to challenge the passage of ships upon the surface. Special ships have been designed for landing troops and heavy military equipment on hostile open beaches. Aircraft have become powerful factors in the control of the sea and of lands beyond the seas. Submarines propelled by nuclear energy can remain beneath the surface for months at a stretch. Rockets with nuclear warheads can be launched from beneath the water's surface. These and other technological advances have radically modified and continue to modify the military properties of oceanic space.

If attention is directed to one set of environmental factors—oceanic space, in the example just above—the change in the range of possible activities appears as an adaptation to a stable environment. But such adaptation appears, from a different perspective, to consist of alterations in another set of environmental factors—modes of transportation and design of weapons, in the example—alterations which change the social meaning or properties or implications of environmental factors which themselves may not have undergone any significant structural change.

Another point of confusion, likewise implicit in the

foregoing paragraphs, is frequent failure to recognize that what is possible to achieve depends not only on properties of the milieu but also on the operational characteristics of the environed unit. This point is most easily appreciated when that unit is a single individual. Knowledge and technique affect the level of performance. A piano is an inert mass of metal, wood, felt, and plastic, until someone plays on it. The quality of the piano sets limits to what the finest pianist can achieve. But an accomplished pianist can produce better music on any given piano than a mere tyro can. A knowledgeable and skillful farmer can produce better crops than can his ignorant neighbor on similar land.

The operational characteristics of the environed unit are no less important, though generally more difficult to identify and evaluate, when that unit is a complex social organization, such as a government department, a fleet or an army, a government as a whole, or an entire political community. Then the internal structure and characteristics of the unit may include a very wide range of factors: for example, the quantity, variety, and quality of the human skills available; the mode of making decisions; the level of loyalty and morale, and many other variables. All these may have a bearing on the organization's capacity (always operating through its human agents) both to set potentially attainable goals and then to achieve them. Relevant knowledge and diplomatic skills are essential attributes of successful statecraft; but the statesman who speaks for a powerful united community is apt to accomplish more than one who represents a nation that is materially weak and internally divided.

We come finally to a still more confused issue, one that derives from failure to observe the *critically important distinction between the relation of environmental factors to decisions and to the operational results of decisions.*

· 93 ·

The widespread failure to observe this distinction may be attributable to the fact that much of the data relevant to the one is also relevant to the other. But the two modes of analysis are not thereby identical or even similar. The perspective of the analyst, the kinds of questions he asks, the explanatory propositions he brings to bear, and the answers that his analysis yields, are as different as day is different from night. We shall return to this issue later in the context of international political analysis. But first there is need to clarify the issue at the level of theory.

Historically, as previously indicated, possibilism represented a revolt against the denial of free will implicit in strict determinism. From the outset, freedom of choice was a central tenet of the possibilist doctrine, at both the philosophical and the empirical level. The reason is obvious. *To admit that choices as well as the operational results of choices may be limited by the milieu is to reintroduce the most repugnant feature of strict determinism.*

In a possibilistic mode of analysis there has to be an undertaking, else there can be no outcome to explain or to predict. But choices, decisions, projects, and undertakings are treated as *givens,* not as behavior to be accounted for. An analyst may make any assumptions, formulate any hypotheses, or carry out any investigations he desires, with respect to the values, motivations, cognition, and decisional behavior of the individual or group whose accomplishments are being investigated. He might conclude, for example, that the actors in the case are motivated by Christian charity, or by pecuniary greed, or by lust for power, or by some other scheme of values. He might conclude that they either do or do not possess adequate knowledge of the environing conditions relevant to their choices and decisions. He might conclude that they behave rationally or irrationally in their assessments of the opportunities and limitations implicit in their milieu, with respect to whatever ends they may have in view.

The analyst, we repeat, can carry out these or any other intellectual operations he may desire with respect to the actors' values, motivations, cognition, and decisional behavior. *But in doing so he steps outside the possibilist frame of reference.* For possibilism simply posits, with reference to any specified undertaking, that environing factors will affect the operational results; and, further, that these limiting factors may be operative even though they are not perceived and reacted to by the person or persons under consideration.

A simple example will help perhaps to make this distinction more clear and explicit. Suppose a man enters an unlighted street on a very dark night. Concepts and methods of behavioral analysis may help to explain how he happens to be there (that is, his motivation and intent), what he imagines the layout of the street to be (his cognition of his milieu), and how he gropes his way forward in the total darkness (his decisions and implementing actions). But there is an open manhole half a block away, directly in his path. He does not know it is there. He cannot perceive it in the darkness. It forms no part of his psycho-milieu (that is, the milieu as he imagines it to be). He cannot react to the unperceived open manhole. Nevertheless, that manhole is a strategic factor in his operational environment, for he will fall into it if he continues on his present course. The unperceived factor sets a limit on the outcome, or operational result, of the man's undertaking. This limitation operates irrespective of his cognition of it in advance. Indeed, his ignorance of the unperceived factor makes it all the more likely to be operative, since his ignorance excludes any possibility of taking adaptive countermeasures in time.

This hypothetical incident has direct relevance to the

applicability and utility of the possibilist frame of reference to international political analysis. The paths of politics are strewn with unperceived open manholes, metaphorically speaking. That is to say, political decisions are constantly taken, and have to be taken, on the basis of incomplete or inaccurate knowledge of conditions of the milieu in which the statesman is operating. This is true of all politics. It is conspicuously and continuously true of diplomatic negotiations, military operations, subversive conspiracy, and most other aspects of international statecraft. This is so because of the extra effort regularly made to conceal relevant intelligence from adverse parties, and to circulate inaccurate reports in order to mislead and deceive. The student of international politics has constantly to assess the operational consequences of discongruity between the situation as the statesman imagines it to be and the situation as it actually is (or as it would be known to a hypothetical omniscient observer).

Let us emphasize once again: POSSIBILISM IS NOT A FRAME OF REFERENCE FOR EXPLAINING OR PREDICTING DECISIONS OR THE PSYCHOLOGICAL ANTECEDENTS OF DECISIONS. Possibilism does not provide any approach whatever to the explanation or prediction of action *per se,* assertions to the contrary notwithstanding. In the possibilist frame of reference, decisions and undertakings are taken as *given,* not as behavior to be analyzed and explained or predicted.[10]

This conclusion seems to us inescapable. Possibilism arose, as we have pointed out above, in the reaction against environmental determinism. As we have also pointed out, one of the attractions of possibilism, in the

[10] This distinction is rarely emphasized as strongly as we have done; but it *was* made in passing in the discussion of "Determinism and Possibilism," by A. C. Montefiore and W. M. Williams, in *Geographical Studies,* 1955, v. 2, p. 1.

intellectual climate of the early twentieth century, was its explicit postulation of freedom of choice. As Febvre put it, in the passage quoted earlier: "Necessities nowhere; possibilities everywhere; and man is the judge of their use."

If one were to take the opposed position—to argue that the milieu sets limits to what men can attempt as well as to what they can achieve—he would be reintroducing the strict environmental determinism which possibilism was contrived expressly to supplant. For this reason, *there is no escape from the conclusion that possibilism either has no relevance whatever to the explanation or prediction of choices and decisions, OR ELSE IT IS CONCEPTUALLY INDISTINGUISHABLE FROM STRICT DETERMINISM.*[11]

[11] This conclusion, inescapable in our view, is not quite universally accepted. One who rejects it *in toto* is the British geographer A. F. Martin, whose argument seems to us to reflect misunderstanding of the historical origins and central postulate of the possibilist doctrine. See his "The Necessity for Determinism," in *Transactions and Papers,* Institute of British Geographers, 1951, no. 17, pp. 1, 6. Another British geographer, O. H. K. Spate (now at the Australian National University), voices a different sort of objection. He does not deny that possibilism represents historically a reaction against environmental determinism. But he queries: "How do you know that your possibilist views aren't in fact determined by your environment? If we take environment as total environment—cultural as well as physical—it is difficult to see what effective reply there is." He then adds that "in the last resort there will always be the stubborn divergence between those who believe that man is broadly a free agent, and those who believe that his ends and means are chosen for him by God or chance or chemistry." From "How Determined Is Possibilism?" in *Geographical Studies,* 1957, v. 4, pp. 3, 7, 11. However, there seems to be no irreconcilable incompatibility between Spate's position and our own. In reviewing our *Man-Milieu Relationship Hypotheses in the Context of International Politics,* Spate said: "Possibilists may receive a shock when told that, unless possibilism takes aims and decisions as given, it 'is conceptually indistinguishable from determinism.' The moral seems to be that geographers must rethink their methodology more than somewhat." *Geographical Review,* 1958, v. 48, pp. 281*ff.*

POSSIBILISM

Environmental possibilism is generally associated with geography. It is true, as we have noted, that geographers, especially French geographers, introduced the possibilist posture into their discipline early in this century. It is likewise to be noted that early discussions of possibilism in geographic writings focused mainly on man's relations to the nonhuman environment. But the possibilist posture and mode of analysis extend far beyond that aspect of man-milieu relationships. We have noted the similarity of environmental possibilism to its contemporary, the philosophical doctrine of pragmatism. Political geographers and political scientists will doubtless have recognized by now that possibilism also resembles the frame of analysis that is widely used in estimating the military and other capabilities of states,[12] and more generally the geographical distribution of national political potentials in the society of nations. We shall return later to this use of the possibilistic mode of analysis, first in connection with general theories of explanation (Chapter VIII) and prediction (Chapter IX), and finally (in Chapter X) in the specific context of international political analysis.

[12] For a discussion of capability analysis from the standpoint of a political geographer, see S. B. Jones, "The Power Inventory and National Strategy," in *World Politics*, 1954, v. 6, pp. 421*ff;* also the same author's "Possibilism and Strategic Thought," in *Annals*, Association of American Geographers, 1954, v. 44, pp. 219*f.*

6

PROBABILISTIC MODELS OF BEHAVIOR

THE EXPOSITION of environmental possibilism in the preceding chapter was directed to the problem of relating environmental factors to operational results, outcomes, performance, and accomplishments. In that discussion it was repeatedly emphasized that the possibilistic mode of analysis provides *no approach whatever to the problem* of relating environmental factors to psychological behavior. For that purpose a different perspective and different frame of analysis are required. In this chapter we examine one of these: the analytic mode based upon probabilistic models of behavior.

It is essential at the outset to recognize explicitly that probabilistic modes of analysis and interpretation are not restricted to behavior. Much of anyone's reasoning about human affairs, in the possibilistic frame or any other, is also essentially probabilistic in a certain sense. For example, if one predicts that no congested urban society could survive attack by thermonuclear weapons, he is in effect asserting that the odds run strongly against survival in that contingency. This, we repeat, is essentially a probabilistic mode of speaking about operational results. We shall return to that issue in Chapters VIII and IX. In the present chapter, however, it is proposed to confine our attention to the function of environmental ideas in probabilistic models of psychological *states* (values, preferences, moods, attitudes, perception, cognition, recognition) and *actions* (choices, decisions, undertakings).[1]

[1] The issue discussed in this chapter was introduced a few years ago in a sequence of statements regarding environmental theories. In an essay comparing the environmental postures of Toynbee and

In explaining psychological states and actions, one is dealing not with conditions and events external to, and concretely separable from, the individual human being whose behavior is being analyzed. One is concerned rather with some kind of psychological interaction between the individual's felt needs and stored knowledge, on the one hand, and the signals or messages conveyed to him via his sensory organs, on the other. That is to say, what matters in shaping human attitudes and decisions (and in explaining and predicting these) is not how the "real world" actually is, but rather how it is perceived and reacted to by the individual in question. In the terminology outlined in Chapter II, what matters here is the individual's psycho-milieu, not his operational milieu.

When the task is to explain a decision made in the past, it may be possible to reconstruct more or less plausibly the psychological behavior that actually occurred. This procedure breaks down if the necessary historical evidence has been destroyed or is for other reasons inaccessible. The procedure will not work at all, of course, when the task is to predict decisions. Then the alternative to sheer speculation is to draw inferences on the basis of the individual's probable conformity to some hypothetical

Huntington, O. H. K. Spate suggested, more or less in passing, that the historic disputation among geographers over environmental determinism vs. freedom of choice could be resolved by a philosophical posture that he called "probabilism." "Toynbee and Huntington: A Study in Determinism," in *Geographical Journal*, London, 1952, v. 118, pp. 406ff. Later, in a lecture at Cambridge University, Spate took this theme a step further. The issue, he said, "is often not so much a matter of all-or-nothing choice or compulsion, but a balance of probabilities." "How Determined Is Possibilism?" in *Geographical Studies*, 1957, v. 4, pp. 3, 20. Still later, in a review of our *Man-Milieu Relationship Hypotheses in the Context of International Politics*, Spate intimated that we had taken his suggestion "rather more seriously than . . . intended." "The End of an Old Song? The Determinism-Possibilism Problem," in *Geographical Review*, 1958, v. 48, p. 281.

norm. This amounts to reasoning from a "model" of typical, or normally expectable, behavior.

Such a model may be simple or complex. It may be set forth explicitly or (more likely) left implicit. A speaker may deny that he has any model in mind at all. Such denials are largely quibbles over words: for most explanations of past choices and decisions, and every prediction that is more than a throw of the dice, are based on some set of assumptions as to what is normally expectable behavior in the milieu and contingency under consideration.

This approach to the explanation and prediction of purposeful behavior is better understood in certain fields than in others. Anthropologists have derived more or less explicit models of behavioral norms prevailing in particular societies. Economists have long accepted explicit models of the typical "economic man." Certain political theories rest upon models of "human nature" as posited in typical "political man."

The discipline of geography exhibits a somewhat different history with regard to behavioral models. In the heyday of environmentalism, writings in human geography showed considerable concern with the choices which led to various areal distributions and patterns. As the possibilist doctrine displaced environmentalism, attention was directed increasingly to the outcomes, or operational results, of *given* choices, rather than to the choices themselves. In fact, as pointed out in the preceding chapter, the possibilist frame of reference offers no approach whatever to explanation of choices and decisions, without reintroducing the deterministic posture that possibilism was specifically intended to supplant. Re-reading some of the theoretical and empirical literature of geography published in the 1920's and 1930's leaves us with two impressions: (1) that the vogue of possibilism divided geographers over the issue of whether choices and decisions were their proper concern at all;[2] and (2) that most geographers, in their empirical work, felt a need for some escape from the narrow confines of possibilism. Many resolved this felt need by explaining and predicting choices by means of (generally implicit) assumptions of normally expectable behavior in the milieu under consideration. This seems to us the essence of Spate's idea of probabilism, though (so far as we are aware) he was the first to use that term in the specific context of geographic theory.

To this day one occasionally encounters political scientists, geographers, and more frequently historians, who insist that every human being is unique, and hence that human choices and decisions are unpredictable. But we

[2] The idea that geographers should concern themselves with choices as well as with the geographical consequences of choices seems to us to have been clearly implicit in the hotly debated thesis of the American geographer H. H. Barrows, whose presidential address to the Association of American Geographers in 1922 pleaded for defining "geography as human ecology" in its areal setting. *Annals,* A.A.G., 1923, v. 13, pp. 1*ff.* Much the same idea was expressed by the British geographer P. M. Roxby, who defined human geography as the study of "the adjustment of human groups to their physical environment. . . ." "The Scope and Aims of Human Geography," in *Scottish Geographical Magazine,* 1930, v. 46, pp. 276, 283. The controversial issue of choice, with its strong environmentalistic overtones, drew firm protests from some of the leading theorists. C. O. Sauer went so far, in 1927, as virtually to read the issue out of geography altogether by reducing man to the status of a mere "agent in the fashioning of the landscape." "Recent Developments in Cultural Geography," in *Recent Developments in the Social Sciences,* edited by E. C. Hayes, Lippincott, 1927, p. 186. Later, he reiterated even more emphatically that "human geography . . . unlike psychology and history, is a science that has nothing to do with individuals but only with human institutions, or cultures." "Foreword to Historical Geography," in *Annals,* A.A.G., 1941, v. 31, pp. 1, 7. Richard Hartshorne, in his exhaustive examination of *The Nature of Geography,* Association of American Geographers, 1939, pp. 120-26, took a less extreme view, but he too saw risks in defining geography as a "science of relations" between man and his milieu, in part lest it "wind up in the dead-end street of environmental determinism."

have noticed that such persons generally do not hesitate, for example, to cross a busy street when the traffic light turns green. In stepping from the curb, they are making an implicit prediction that adverse traffic will obey the signal. In effect such a prediction is simply an inference (usually, though not always, subconscious) from a generalized model (rarely articulated) as to how a "typical" motorcar driver behaves in the given milieu. The pedestrian usually knows nothing specific about the personalities of the particular drivers of oncoming cars. Nor does he usually know anything about their individual driving habits. But he does have some notion of how drivers generally behave in that city and country; and he predicts an individual driver's behavior on the expectation of probable conformity to that hypothetical norm.

What we have just been describing are the rock-bottom elements of what is commonly called a behavioral model. Such a model is probabilistic in the sense that it embodies assumptions as to what is normally expectable behavior in the given environmental context. That is all any behavioral model ever provides. The model never provides a description of any specific individual's behavior. It carries no built-in assumption that the generalized description of average behavior fits any particular person. *No behavioral model can possibly anticipate idiosyncratic deviations from the hypothetical norm.*[8]

Such norms are derived by generalizing from past observations. Such an empirical generalization is initially no more than a trial hypothesis. When (in the example given above) further observation confirms that motor vehicle drivers almost invariably do obey traffic signals, the hypothesis is said to be confirmed or verified to a high

[8] On the ubiquity of models both in daily living and in more formal study of human affairs, see K. W. Deutsch, *The Nerves of Government*, Free Press, 1963, ch. 1, especially p. 13.

degree of probability. In due course, the confirmed hypothesis evolves into an assumption accepted without further proof, and eventually hardens into a firm expectation reflected in strongly patterned habitual behavior. At any stage in the evolution from trial hypothesis to habit-conditioned response, the proposition may serve as the general premise (sometimes called "explanatory hypothesis" or "explanatory law") from which past behavior may be accounted for or future behavior predicted by logical deduction.

This approach to choices and decisions is more often implicitly than explicitly employed. Two British geographers, S. W. Wooldridge and W. G. East, put the issue as follows: Suppose a geographer is asked to "account for" the distribution of population in a particular country. He cannot undertake to identify and analyze "the myriad individual decisions which entered, unrecorded and unexplained, into the making of the settlement pattern. We still, in a sense, account for what we describe in pointing out that the population groups itself in accord with economic potentialities, within the range of our present resources. . . . All that is implied is that in a local and temporary sense man disposes himself and his structures and fabrications in sites and situations which are *rational,* or which at least appear to be so. . . . We follow their *natural* thoughts and reactions as we note their distribution of their material culture" (italics added).[4]

Now, before commenting further on this method of explaining decisions, let us examine an application of it to a specific (and quite typical) geographic problem. We have chosen for this purpose a section from J. C. Weaver's analysis and interpretation of changing patterns in the use

[4] S. W. Wooldridge and W. G. East, *The Spirit and Purpose of Geography,* Hutchinson, London, 1951, pp. 33-34.

of cropland in the American Middle West.[5] One of the problems in this research project was to account for an observed shift in the crop pattern of a marginal farming area in southern Illinois. Weaver's research revealed that the soil of the area was thin, poorly drained, and under-lain with impervious clay hardpan; that the land was worked mainly by more or less transient tenant farmers; and that soybeans had displaced corn as the dominant crop. Here is Weaver's explanation: When a new strain of soybean, "especially suited to the ecological conditions" of the area, became available, "the claypan farmers *were quick to discover* that here was a crop capable of making an at least modest return on their long untreated soils. . . . Because of the impervious claypan and the failure of moisture to drain easily downward into the sub-soil, rainy springs mean waterlogged topsoil and delayed planting. Reasonable returns are far more likely from soy-beans following late seeding than is the case with corn." In addition to these and other "physical advantages . . . were a *variety of strong economic inducements* . . . a cash crop which yielded its return almost before the [farmer's] bill for seed came due . . . a safe cash re-turn with a minimum of outlay . . . for land improve-ment," a consideration especially attractive to tenant farmers who "may cultivate a piece of land for no more than one year" (italics added).

In the technique described by Wooldridge and East, and applied by Weaver, the analyst deduces from a state of affairs the *probable* human motives, environmental knowledge, and psychological processes from which the given state of affairs was derived. Weaver did not under-take to reconstruct specifically and in detail the "myriad individual decisions [in the words of Wooldridge and

[5] J. C. Weaver, "Changing Patterns of Cropland Use in the Middle West," in *Economic Geography*, 1954, v. 30, pp. 1, 45ff.

East] which entered, unrecorded and unexplained" into the making of the observed pattern. Instead, his "explanation" consists of inferences from a partially articulated model of the typical tenant farmer's presumed behavior in the context of the problem.

In the problem cited, the analyst's behavioral assumptions—partly explicit, partly implicit—seem to be about as follows: first, it was assumed that the farmers in question desired to earn money, and would plant those crops which seemed likely to bring the highest return with the least effort and risk. Second, it was assumed that the farmers were informed about farming in general and about the local conditions in particular. Third, it was assumed that they acted more or less rationally in deciding what crops would yield the highest return with the least risk in the given milieu.

In making such assumptions, no claim was made that all the farmers in the area actually behaved precisely this way. It was simply intimated that these assumptions were close enough approximations on the average to enable the geographer to draw probably tenable conclusions as to how the process in question probably occurred. Here we would call attention to the similarity of such probabilistic models of behavior with the so-called statistical determinism described in Chapter III (see page 66, above).

Speaking more generally, the number and complexity of the assumptions which an analyst puts into his behavioral model will depend on his judgment as to what is necessary for a satisfactory explanation or basis of prediction. But so far as we are aware, every such model which pertains to more or less deliberative decisions (that is, not merely to a conditioned reflex) includes at the very least: (1) assumptions as to the actor's motivation and intent, (2) assumptions as to the quantity and quality of his knowledge of the milieu in which he is operating, and

(3) assumptions as to his mode of utilizing such knowledge in defining alternatives and taking decisions.

Ideological or other characteristics of the model, it is clear, depend on the substantive content of these assumptions. Assumptions regarding motivation, for example, can have an acquisitive, power-seeking, self-denying, philanthropic, or other content. Assumptions regarding the actor's knowledge of his milieu can range anywhere from total ignorance to total knowledge of relevant environing factors. Assumptions regarding the mode of utilizing environmental knowledge in making decisions can be that the hypothetical "typical" person is predominantly rational or that his behavior is explicable by some other mode of decision-making.

A familiar version of behavioral model, derived largely, one suspects, from classical economics, might be called "common-sense probabilism." In this ubiquitous but rarely articulated model, men are presumed to be predominantly acquisitive, adequately knowledgeable, and generally rational. In the context of daily living, the assumption of acquisitiveness usually shows a strong pecuniary coloration. People are assumed to want money and the things money can buy. Second, in common-sense probabilism people are assumed generally to have environmental knowledge that is adequate for their purposes. That is to say, the actor's psycho-milieu is assumed to fit in essential respects the operational milieu in which his decisions are executed. Third, the common-sense probabilist assumes that the individual applies his environmental knowledge rationally to the choice of ends achievable with the means at his command and to the choice of appropriate available means to achieve attainable ends. That is to say, he estimates rationally the opportunities and limitations implicit in his milieu. Finally, built into common-sense probabilism is the implicit assumption that the actor upon the field, so to speak, and the analyst who observes (or researches) from the sideline both perceive and evaluate the milieu of the actor in substantially the same way.

Some such behavioral model, we submit, is implicit in Griffith Taylor's so-called "scientific determinism" and in the rhetoric of nearly everyone who employs deterministic or environmentalistic modes of speaking (as exhibited in Chapters III and IV). Let us consider Taylor's familiar example of Antarctica as a milieu which (he claims) *largely determines* man's *choices* and *actions* with reference to it. The purport of what he says is about as follows: *If* the choice of effective means to a desired end in a given milieu is narrowly circumscribed (as in establishing permanent settlements in Antarctica), and *if* (as Taylor explicitly assumes) persons involved in the enterprise are adequately cognizant of limitations implicit in that milieu, and *if* (as he also appears to assume) such persons take their environmental knowledge rationally into account in making decisions, *then* it follows that there will be close correlation between environmental limits and human decisions in relation thereto.

If, as the common-sense probabilist also appears generally to assume, the analyst's own knowledge of the milieu in question and his own mode of thinking about it correspond in essential respects to his subject's, then the analyst can explain the subject's past decisions and predict his probable future decisions simply by imagining how a "rational man" *like himself* would react to the milieu in question.

Thus, starting with a given action in the past and the set of environmental factors which he deems to be relevant, the probabilistic analyst reasons backwards to account for the action, as indicated above. Alternatively, starting with a set of environing factors, he reasons forward to predictions of probable psychological responses thereto. This, we submit, is substantially the purport of most statements, examples of which were quoted in Chapter IV, in which environmental factors are asserted to "determine" or to "influence" choices, decisions, and undertakings.

When not construed as naïve teleology or as poetic license, such statements say in substance that the environed persons or group *envisaged* certain ends; that they *perceived and comprehended* adequately the opportunities and limitations latent in their milieu; and that they applied such knowledge *rationally* in choosing ends that were possible and in formulating means appropriate to the ends selected.

This kind of probabilistic model of behavior carries an implicit assumption that the environed individual or group is capable of choosing among alternatives. But that is NOT equivalent to assuming that *all* choices which, by definition, are *possible* choices are *equally probable* choices. THE ESSENCE OF SUCH A MODEL IS THAT SOME CHOICES ARE MORE PROBABLE THAN OTHERS. The function of the model is to enable the analyst to sort the more probable choices from the less probable, or to arrange a set of choices on a sort of scale of estimated degrees of probability. By reference to the assumptions of normally expectable behavior, incorporated into the model, the analyst eliminates as very improbable or as somewhat less improbable those choices which would represent greater or lesser deviations from the hypothetical norm.

The reliability of conclusions derived by inference from models of typical, or normally expectable, behavior varies widely. In the rest of this chapter, we shall consider some, though certainly not all, of the limiting conditions.

Every assumption built into a model of normally expectable behavior must satisfy the test of social context. For example, an assumption that economic gain takes precedence over other motives may be valid in one context but not in another. This is illustrated by studies in the 1930's in which it was predicted that migration to California would soon decline. Those predictions were based mainly on the assumptions that desire for economic gain was the principal motive for migration; and that economic opportunities in California would not sustain continued large-scale migration on that basis. Yet migration to California did continue on a scale that could not possibly be explained on economic grounds alone. Leaving aside the economic stimulus later provided by World War II, one investigator concluded that the earlier predictions failed to take sufficiently into account the extent to which "amenities" of living—congenial climate in particular—had come to compete with economic gain as a high-priority value in American society.[6] In short, analysis of the human response to a given milieu had misfired because the analyst accepted too readily the common-sense assumption of economic motivation.

Another complicating factor in the construction of satisfactory behavioral models is what certain geographers have called the "legacy of the past."[7] One facet of this drag is the factor of habit, or accustomed ways of doing things. In some settings, habit may compete successfully with both knowledge and rationality. For example, after the forests were logged-off in northern Michigan early in this century, thousands of destitute settlers moved into the cheap cut-over lands. They brought with them a stock of farming lore that had worked well enough in a more

[6] See E. L. Ullmann, "Amenities as a Factor in Regional Growth," in *Geographical Review*, 1954, v. 44, pp. 119*ff*.

[7] We are indebted, for this phrase, to the British geographer A. A. L. Caesar of Cambridge University.

favorable farming milieu, but proved to be ill suited to the sandy soils, frequent summer droughts, and short growing season of northern Michigan. Yet efforts of agricultural experts to introduce new crops and to persuade the sand-hill farmers to try them, and to modify their tillage in specified rational ways, met all too often with stolid and stubborn resistance to change. One of us can remember, as a child, hearing his father, the village banker, plead with the farmers to accept the experts' advice, and their usual rejoinder: "They may be right, but I never did it that way."

Another facet of the legacy of the past is the cost of modernization. This drag seems to be heaviest in periods of rapid technological change. Cities outgrow their streets and other facilities, yet little is done to relieve congestion. Obsolescent mines and factories are deemed too useful to scrap, even when no longer able to compete with newer installations. Ships and railroad equipment become obsolete long before they wear out. Politicians and businessmen alike may recoil from the high cost of replacement, and make do with increasing difficulties, especially in the longer-industrialized countries.

Discussions of foreign policy and of foreign-policy making very commonly exhibit the characteristics which we identified above as a sort of "common-sense probabilism." Underlying assumptions are often obscured in environmentalistic rhetoric, as in the numerous examples previously cited. But scratch the surface, so to speak, of almost any discussion of foreign policy or the conduct of foreign relations, and one is apt to discover the familiar premises that men are predominantly acquisitive, adequately knowledgeable, and generally rational.

In the specific context of foreign policy, the assumption of acquisitiveness is typically translated into the closely related concept of power orientation. Politics is said to be a "struggle for power." Desire to enhance the power of one's own state over others is said to be the paramount objective of the foreign policies of all states. This concept of national interest, this assumption as to motivation and purpose, has fascinated American students of international politics over the last quarter of a century or more. It is often dogmatically asserted as if it were a self-evident law of nature.

Whether this assumption is adequately descriptive of typical, normally expectable policy-making behavior is debatable, to say the least. The term *power*, as carefully noted in Chapter II, is heavily laden with connotations of violence, force, coercion, and threats thereof. No amount of defining and redefining seems to make the slightest dent on the way people generally construe the term *power*. To posit maximization of power as the top-priority objective of statecraft is, therefore, in effect, to posit maximization of capacity to use violence as the top-priority objective. The consequence is to exaggerate the relative importance of military factors in international politics. Excessive stress on power orientation may also obscure, as well as divert attention from, the diversity and multiplicity of purposes and projects which characterize the statecraft of every government. Furthermore, the pure-power, or near pure-power, assumption of national interest does not provide a plausible basis for explaining the actions of the militarily weaker but increasingly more influential states which comprise so large and important a sector of the society of nations today.

Whether or not the reader accepts our objections to the uncritical assumption of power orientation, the main point at issue here is that *some* concept of national interest, some set of assumptions regarding purposes to be accomplished, is embodied in all explanations and predictions of foreign policy and of policy-making behavior. What the analyst assumes about the purposes of statesmen will almost certainly affect his assumptions as to what environmental factors probably were (or probably will be) taken into account in particular policy-making situations.

Turning to the issue of cognition and evaluation of the milieu, there seems to be a general tendency to assume that statesmen and their staffs normally command *effectively* a stock of information that is sufficiently complete and reliable for the purposes which they envisage. This assumption is implicit in the venerable cliché that "politics is the art of the possible." This old saw is sometimes quoted as a description of typical policy-making behavior, sometimes as a precept for policy-makers. In either context, it implies that those who make decisions for the state can be presumed as a rule to know what projects are feasible in a given milieu and what strategies are likely to be most effective.

This may prove to be an untenable assumption in many instances. It is one thing to assume that farmers usually know the elements of good farming in a given milieu, a premise derived by averaging the behavior of many farmers (see page 106, above). It is certainly more dubious to assume that any specific farmer commands such knowledge. If that is so, how much more dubious it must be to assume that a specific head of government, or foreign minister, or legislative body, or other decisional unit commands *effectively* the vastly wider range of information, much of it extremely technical and complex, that is required to conduct foreign relations effectively and to provide an adequate military defense in conditions prevailing in the domestic and international milieu.

The higher one moves in the hierarchy of a complex government, the more one is impressed by the remoteness of the ultimate decision-makers from the operational milieu in which their decisions are executed. What passes for knowledge of the situation (the milieu) at the higher levels consists usually of more or less generalized descriptions and abstracts, several stages removed from on-the-spot observations. On most issues the individual or group responsible for a major decision will have little time and only rather general background of information with which to check what is prepared at lower working levels of the organization.

Let us assume (and we think it is an obviously tenable assumption) that the British decision to send military forces to reoccupy the Suez Canal in 1956 was predicated on a firm expectation that the job could be finished quickly. How did Prime Minister Eden and those in whom he confided presumably come to such a conclusion, which turned out to be so radically discongruent with reality? One can only speculate, of course. Our own speculation would be that they probably received estimates of the situation from various sources. Such estimates probably included, among other things, statements regarding the strength and deployment of British and French military forces, their state of readiness, landing craft and other transport and handling equipment available, liaison arrangements with the French command, the state of Egyptian military defenses, the morale of Egyptian troops and civil population, the probable behavior of other governments and peoples, etc. In addition, one may perhaps assume that Eden himself had some general notions of his own regarding Near Eastern countries and peoples, regarding British military prowess, and the like. But is it credible to assume that he had much fresh knowledge of any of the relevant matters, or the time necessary to check up on his experts?

These questions immediately suggest others. To what extent is a top-level executive a virtual prisoner of the civil and military officials who brief him? On the other hand, to what extent may his known prejudices and pre-suppositions affect the substance and verbal coloration of what his subordinates choose to tell him? To what extent do their own cultural biases color and distort what they perceive and the importance which they attach thereto? To what extent do such considerations affect the whole chain of communications in a complex decision-making organization?

These and similar questions that will come to mind raise doubts as to the presumptive tenability of the assumption that those who make decisions for the state always, or even generally, really know as much as they are presumed to know about the milieu in which they are operating. The view that they do is clearly a hypothesis, to be confirmed by evidence, if possible—rarely, if ever, to be uncritically taken for granted. However, in the absence of specific confirmatory evidence, the foreign policy analyst may have no alternative but to proceed on some assumption as to the manner in which information is normally gathered, interpreted, and communicated upward through the organization under consideration.

We come, finally, to the closely related question of how images of the milieu are utilized in reaching policy decisions. Here most students of international politics will probably regard as inadequate the common-sense assumption that deliberate choices and decisions generally reflect rational definition of attainable ends and rational formulation of strategies most likely to be effective. Are intellectual processes sufficiently similar, in general, under different conditions—linguistic, ideological, institutional, etc.—to justify generalized assumptions applicable to all governments? Or does one need a typology that distinguishes decision-making in various categories of governments? On what basis would such a typology yield the most reliable conclusions? Communist *vs.* non-communist systems? Totalitarian *vs.* non-totalitarian systems? Authoritarian *vs.* democratic systems? Parliamentary democratic *vs.* non-parliamentary democratic systems? Or does one need a separate model for every government, based on observations through time? One can carry the process of analytic reduction to the level of specific persons and groups, in which case he will have moved out of the probabilistic frame of reference altogether.[8] We cannot go further at this point with these questions, but we shall return to some of them later in the context of more general theories of explanation and prediction.

[8] There may be cogent reasons for studying specific entities as discrete "wholes," as Hartshorne argues in *Perspective on the Nature of Geography,* Rand-McNally, 1959, p. 157, and elsewhere.

7

THE COGNITIVE ASPECT OF MAN-
MILIEU RELATIONSHIPS

PROBABILISTIC MODELS can never rise above the assumptions from which they are derived—assumptions regarding what is typical or normally expectable behavior
in the contingencies to which the model relates. As indicated in the preceding chapter, such assumptions are derived from empirical generalizations of past observation
and experience. These assumptions, as was also noted, frequently embody vaguely articulated expectations deeply
rooted in the common culture, and express the so-
called "common sense" of that society.[1] But evidence
confronts one on all sides that "common-sense" assumptions may be less than adequate to explain and predict
decisions taken in various particular contexts, especially
those of individuals and groups functioning in formal
roles in complex organizations. Thus there is an ever-
present need for more factual data both to fashion better
models, and also to describe and explain the specific behavior of particular decision-makers in specified settings.

One discovers a considerable range of approaches to
this task. At one pole is the traditional mode of historical
research, which utilizes a minimum of formal conceptual-
ization. At the other pole one finds an assortment of conceptual schemes and analytical modes designed to achieve
more orderly and insightful research and interpretation.
The focus in the present chapter is on the ecological as-

[1] This issue is discussed by Michael Scriven in "Truisms as the
Grounds for Historical Explanations," in *Theories of History*,
edited by Patrick Gardiner, Free Press, 1959, pp. 443*ff*.

pect of these more specifically empirical concepts and theories.

Our point of departure is the generally accepted thesis that a person's conscious and purposive responses to his milieu are explicable only in terms of psychological events, identified by such words as perception, recognition, selection, reaction, mood, attitude, choice, decision, etc. A person's values and other psychological predispositions direct his attention selectively to certain features of his milieu; and he interprets what he selectively perceives in the light of conscious memories and subconscious stored experience. We shall use the term *cognitive behavioralism* to designate the thesis that a person consciously responds to his milieu as he apperceives it.[2]

The approach to man-milieu relationships through the specific cognitive behavior of particular individuals is designed, as indicated above, to overcome in some degree the shortcomings of inference from general models of normally expectable behavior. Instead of drawing conclusions regarding an individual's *probable* motivations and purposes, his environmental knowledge, and his intellectual processes linking purposes and knowledge, on the basis of *assumptions* as to the way people are likely on the average to behave in a given social context, the cognitive behavioralist—be he narrative historian or systematic social scientist—undertakes to find out as precisely as possible how specific persons actually did perceive and respond in particular contingencies.

Speaking generally, cognitive behavioralism bypasses

[2] Perhaps a more expressive label for this cognitive posture towards man-milieu relationships would be *cognitive environmentalism*. We would favor this term but for one consideration. *Environmentalism* is so tightly linked (especially in the intellectual history of the geography discipline) with teleological imagery and connotations that any term containing that word would almost certainly be offensive as well as confusing.

COGNITIVE ASPECT

the dualism which postulates man and milieu as separate
entities linked together by mysterious "chains of cause
and effect," a concept that lurks persistently in deterministic and environmentalistic rhetoric and teleological
metaphors. If rigorously consistent, the cognitive behavioralist disregards the so-called "real world" external to
the environed individual or decisional group. That real
world may exist, but its "true" characteristics are unknown and unknowable to the environed individuals. The
milieu to which their values, desires, moods, attitudes,
deliberations, choices, decisions, and undertakings are related is the milieu which is experienced through selective
perception and interpreted in the light of past experience.

This milieu-as-apperceived is sometimes called the subjective environment to distinguish it from the "real world,"
which is called the objective or geographic environment.
It is also called the behavioral environment: that is the
environment to which the individual responds. This concept of environment as perceived and reacted to approx-
imates the "life space" and "field" concepts of social psychology. Kurt Lewin, one of the pioneers in this area,
defined the "life space" as "the person and the psychological environment as it exists for him." In another context he said: "Psychology has to view the life space, including the person and his environment, as one field." [8]

For reasons reviewed above (pp. 28ff), it seems to us
less confusing to call this concept simply the psycho-

[8] *Field Theory in Social Science,* Selected Theoretical Papers by
Kurt Lewin, edited by Dorwin Cartright, Harper, 1951, pp. xi, 57,
240, and *passim.* Describing Lewin's work, Morton Deutscher says:
"The most fundamental construct for Lewin is that of the psychological 'field' or life space . . . which consists of the person and
his environment viewed as *one* constellation of interdependent
factors." "Field Theory in Social Psychology," in *Handbook of
Social Psychology,* edited by Gardner Lindzey, Addison-Wesley,
1954, v. 1, pp. 182, 185.

milieu. This concept of the milieu-as-apperceived (that is, as perceived and reacted to) must not be confused with the operational milieu, generally called the "geographic environment" by psychologists. The former provides data for the explanation of decisions and other psychological events; the latter, for the explanation of operational results of decisions, or "achievements," defined by one psychologist as a "generic term for the relationships better than chance existing between, and due to, an organism and variables in its . . . geographical surroundings" viewed in historical and future as well as present perspective.[4]

The approach to behavioral analysis through the concept of psycho-milieu, the milieu as apperceived, is well recognized is historiography. Many, perhaps most, historians would accept the familiar passage on this issue by the British philosopher R. C. Collingwood: "The fact that certain people live, for example, on an island has in itself no effect on their history; what has an effect is the way they conceive of that position. . . . In itself [insularity] is merely a raw material for historical activity, and the character of historical life depends on how this raw material is used."[5]

The same thesis was argued, in terms of the same example, the fact and the idea of insularity, by Lucien Febvre, the aggressive French exponent of environmental possibilism (see page 83, above): ". . . when we see how rashly some writers are always sketching a type of islander for whom the free wind is as a perpetual call from the distant unknown, and from constant contem-

[4] Egon Brunswik, "The Probability Point of View," ch. 12 of *Psychological Theory: Contemporary Readings,* edited by M. H. Marx, Macmillan, 1951, p. 188.

[5] R. C. Collingwood, *The Idea of History,* Oxford University Press, 1946, p. 200.

plation of the sea enlarges his horizon to embrace the ocean, whilst others (or sometimes the same) with the same boldness, embroider ingenious variations on the theme of isolation . . . it is not geography, but psychology, to which we are paying homage. For what finally matters is the idea adopted by the people—the political group—with regard to their geographical position . . . though this idea may be quite wrong or have no basis in reality." [6]

To Collingwood's and Febvre's thesis, the geographer O. H. K. Spate has replied that "people cannot conceive of their insular position in any way unless they live on an island." [7]

If one generalizes Spate's rejoinder, the result is a thesis which is contradicted by a great deal of authenticated evidence. How many oil wells have been driven where no oil existed? How many farmers have tried to grow crops unsuited to particular soils and climates? How many ships have piled-up on reefs and shoals incorrectly marked in navigational charts? How many military campaigns have failed because of erroneous notions of topographic, climatic, or other obstacles to be overcome?

From time beyond memory, people have formed opinions and shaped their actions on the basis of images that bore little or no resemblance to reality. One thoroughly investigated exhibit of such discongruity and its consequences was the now all-but-forgotten panic produced in

[6] Lucien Febvre, *A Geographical Introduction to History*, translated from the French, Knopf, 1925, p. 225. This thesis is frequently reiterated by historians and philosophers of history. Typical is the following excerpt from a BBC lecture by the British historian David Thomson: "It is not a river itself that matters as a geographic feature; it is whether the inhabitants of both banks think of it as a main artery of their common life, or as a 'natural frontier' between them." *The Listener*, London, May 5, 1960, v. 63, p. 780.

[7] O. H. K. Spate, "Toynbee and Huntington: A Study in Determinism," in *Geographical Journal*, London, 1952, v. 118, p. 423.

1938 by Orson Welles's vivid radio broadcast of an imaginary landing near Princeton, New Jersey, of invaders from Mars. A later example was the epidemic of reports of "flying saucers" in the sky during the later 1940's, when millions of Americans were very jittery about atomic bombs, rockets, and other new gadgets of the dawning nuclear era. To contend that "people cannot conceive of their insular position in any way unless they live on an island" is equivalent to saying that they cannot conceive of nonexistent invaders from outer space or that they cannot imagine they perceive nonexistent flying objects.[8]

An important conclusion can be formulated from such discongruities between image and reality: *With regard to moods, attitudes, preferences, choices, decisions, and undertakings, erroneous ideas of the milieu may be just as influential as ideas that conform to the "realities" of the milieu.* This proposition has received increasing attention from geographers and behavioral scientists. We shall take further note of some of its implications in a moment. But

[8] As the psychologist Kurt Koffka has pointed out, discongruity between image and reality, between what is apperceived and what is there, is the essence of the art of camouflage. He also notes that there is often discongruity with reference to size ("the moon looks large on the horizon and small on the zenith"), motion ("we can see motion when no real motion occurs, as on the cinematographic screen"), etc. "The Gestalt Interpretation of Perception," in *Psychological Theory*, edited by M. H. Marx, Macmillan, 1951, pp. 374-75. The linguistic expert B. L. Whorf characterized as follows the psychological environment of a person ignorant of those aspects of the physical universe which one cannot perceive directly and can conceive only within a frame of scientific theories and inferences: For such a person, "the earth is flat; the sun and moon are shining objects of small size that pop up daily above an eastern rim, move through the upper air, and sink below the western edge. . . . The sky is an inverted bowl made of some blue material. . . . Bodies . . . fall because . . . there is nothing to hold them up. . . . Cooling is not a removal of heat but an addition of 'cold'; leaves are green . . . from the 'greenness' in them." "Language, Mind, and Reality," in *ETC.*, 1952, v. 9, pp. 167, 172.

first, because the evidence of discongruity between image and milieu is so pervasively important, it will be useful to consider a few more instances of it.

First, a few homely examples from a list that could be extended indefinitely: One of us stepped into a Western Union office to send a cablegram to Brussels, *Belgium*. The clerk checked the message, but could not locate Brussels in the rate-book. "Belgium," she said, "that's in Holland, isn't it?" Then there was the American tourist who entered the post office of a French village, to mail a parcel to Boston, Massachusetts. The postmistress, however, refused his parcel, saying: "Boston, Angleterre, oui; Boston, Etats-Unis, ça n'existe pas!" Various maps have appeared which caricature the geographical perspective of people in different American regions. In one of these, entitled "A New Yorker's Idea of the United States of America," the most conspicuous features are Manhattan, Long Island, Cape Cod, and Florida. Great Salt Lake appears as one of the Great Lakes, Nebraska as a small town in Illinois, and the rest is comparably and fantastically jumbled. In another of these caricature maps, entitled "A Texan's Map of the U.S.A.," Texas appears larger than all the other states combined, with most of the north and east labeled "unexplored territory."

When one turns to rather more notable historic examples, there is the decision of the Queen of Spain to finance Columbus to sail westward across the Atlantic to Asia, in ignorance of the geographic layout that rendered the undertaking impossible as conceived and undertaken. For centuries thereafter, men imagined the existence of a "Terra Incognita" somewhere in the distant ocean where they would discover the fabled gold mines of King Solomon. The history of boundary-making provides many examples of discongruity between geographical image and reality. As originally drawn and described, for example, the boundary between the United States and Canada failed to conform in several places to the actual geographic layout. Until nearly the end of the fifteenth century, even presumably well-informed Europeans imagined the Atlantic and Indian oceans to be separate and unconnected bodies of water. Any collection of early maps, arranged in chronological order covering several centuries, will exemplify dramatically how slow and difficult has been the accumulation of even approximately accurate knowledge of the geographical configuration of any region.[9]

Maps are still a prolific source of discongruity between psychological image and geographic reality, not so much because of the map-makers' deficiencies as because of lay ignorance of the properties of map projections. This is not the place to dwell in detail on the technical aspects of map-making. But a few words on this subject may not be out of order since non-geographers often seem to regard maps as visually equivalent to geographic reality. Maps are indispensable aids, of course, to comprehension of the dimensions, distributions, and configuration of the earth's surface. But no design upon a sphere can be transferred to a flat surface without distortion of some or all of its dimensions. This is a favorite theme of geographers, who deplore the uncritical lay use of maps—any old maps —without regard to the properties of the grid on which they are constructed.

Experts may disagree as to what projection is best suited to portray a given problem. But there is no disagreement that the still ubiquitous Mercator world map, which depicts the earth as a rectangle, has profoundly affected

[9] A first-class exhibit of this historical process is *The South-east in Early Maps*, by W. P. Cumming, Princeton University Press, 1958, which contains in chronological sequence a fair sampling of the several hundred maps that depict what was known about the West Indies and adjacent mainland through several centuries following the Columbian discoveries.

people's thinking about international politics. The continents can be centered in various ways on the Mercator map, or the map can be continued horizontally so as to show certain areas more than once. Frequently in American versions of the Mercator map, the United States appears in the center, with the divided halves of Eurasia at the right and left margin. Looking at such a map encourages the illusion that the United States does in fact occupy the central position in world politics. If, however, the map is shifted so that the Soviet Union appears in the middle, with a divided America on the margins, precisely the opposite geo-political illusion is evoked. The fact of the matter, of course, is that neither the Soviet Union nor the United States nor any other country occupies a central position upon the terrestrial globe. The strategic properties of their respective locations depend on the state of weapons, transport, and other aspects of technology, on the patterns of international political relations, and on the kinds of conflict-contingencies envisaged.

As a chart for navigating ships across the ocean, the Mercator map was nearly ideal, especially in the era of sail.[10] As long as European states dominated most of the earth and ships provided the main links connecting continents, the Mercator map was also fairly satisfactory for depicting commercial and military phenomena. A Mercator map, placed with its central north-south axis on the longitude of London, illustrates quite well the geographic structure of British seapower in the nineteenth century.

[10] Not all non-geographers may be aware that the Mercator map was designed as a chart for mariners. Since meridians and parallels on this grid intersect at right angles, as they do on the globe, it follows that a straight line connecting any two points on the map shows the same compass bearing at every point on the line. But such lines, with certain minor exceptions, do not represent the shortest distance between the points. Most "great circles" appear as curved lines on the Mercator map.

As a map to illustrate the intercontinental relations of the Soviet Union and the United States, in an age of jet planes and ballistic missiles, the conventional Mercator map has serious manifest defects. This map does not portray the clustering of Canada and the Soviet Union around the Arctic ocean. Viewed from this map, the elaborate system of American air defenses in northern Canada makes no sense whatever. Likewise, the conventional Mercator map exaggerates the width of the northern reaches of the Atlantic and Pacific oceans, thereby contributing to the historic American illusion of political and military isolation from the Old World.

The record of American statecraft, and books dealing with American foreign policy, contain many exhibits of the spell cast by the Mercator map on even presumably well informed and geographically sophisticated statesmen and scholars. Perhaps the most extreme example of this spell comes from the autobiography of James Frisbie Hoar, Senator from Massachusetts around the turn of the last century. In the debate on the Hawaiian Islands, in 1898, Hoar argued for annexation. Why? Let the Senator tell us in his own words: "Hawaii is 2,100 miles from our Pacific coast. Yet if a line be drawn from the point of our territory nearest Asia [that is, the outermost Aleutian island] to the southern boundary of California, that line being the chord of which our Pacific coast is the bow, Hawaii will fall this side of it." [11] We suggest that the reader try this one out upon a Mercator map and then check the result upon a globe. We think he will agree that Senator Hoar out-Mercatored Mercator!

Much more could be said, if space permitted, regarding the properties of maps on different grids, and their impact on our thinking about international politics. The

[11] G. F. Hoar, *Autobiography of Seventy Years*, Scribner, 1903, v. 2, p. 305.

point that we desire to emphasize is simply that people's attitudes and also the decisions of statesmen are based upon conceptions of geographic reality, and that these in turn appear to depend in no small degree upon the kinds of maps to which they are accustomed.

The general level of geographical knowledge today is undoubtedly higher than ever before. But the knowledge of particular individuals varies enormously, and is often incredibly inaccurate. If anyone doubts this, we suggest that he perform the following experiment: Distribute to any group (not including professional geographers, of course) a blank map of the world, and ask them to draw in the boundaries of the Soviet Union, the principal rivers of Africa, and the line of the so-called Iron Curtain between Eastern and Western Europe; also to locate Saigon, Peking, Moscow, Berlin, and Cairo. We have repeatedly run this sort of experiment on graduate students in the social sciences, with nearly incredible results: for example, Cape Horn confused with the Cape of Good Hope; Suez located at the Strait of Gibraltar; and Moscow located anywhere from the vicinity of Archangel to the shore of the Black Sea.

Often, perhaps much more often, discongruity between psychological image and environmental reality arises not so much from sheer ignorance of the geographic layout, or from uncritical habituation to particular map projections, as from erroneous ideas about other environing factors. The Battle of New Orleans was fought in January 1815, in the mistaken belief that a state of war still existed between Britain and the United States. The Monroe doctrine was promulgated in 1823, with reference to a threat of European military intervention against the former American colonies of Spain, after the threat had already subsided. The British naval base upon the island of Singapore is said to have been designed after World War I on the mistaken assumption that swamps, jungles, and other natural obstacles would prevent any hostile approach in force across the nearby mainland of Malaya. The Battle of the Bulge in World War II caught the Allied High Command unprepared, in December 1944, because of faulty assessment of intelligence reports. American missile and satellite research after World War II proceeded for several years on the basis of widely believed assumptions regarding the backwardness of Russian scientific knowledge and engineering capabilities.

Sometimes a discongruity is the result of an *accustomed perspective* rather than of ignorance or misconception of geographic facts. For example, the terms by which we designate major regions of the earth carry strong overtones of historical political and other relationships. The terms Western Ocean (Atlantic), West Indies, Near East, Far East, etc., all reflect the historic facts of European expansion during past centuries. If the interregional history of the last thousand years had been written from a different geographical perspective, our vocabulary might be considerably different. Suppose the Chinese instead of the Europeans had been the dominant people. America might today be the Far East, and Europe the Far West. Suppose the North American aborigines had explored and settled the rest of the world. The Atlantic might now be the Eastern Ocean; Europe, the Near East; the Near East, the Far East; the Far East, the Far West.

We start our study of international politics, and our politicians, diplomats, civil servants and military officers practice their crafts, with a vocabulary, a set of concepts, and mental images of the milieu, inherited from the era when European peoples controlled or dominated most of the interregional traffic and the political relations of the world. This intellectual equipment, one suspects, constantly affects not only our mode of speaking but also, in subtle and little understood ways, our habits of thinking about places and peoples and about the political and other linkages which bind them together into a global international system.

The British geographer H. J. Mackinder repeatedly emphasized this point. In one connection he said: "The influence of geographical conditions upon human activities has depended . . . not merely on the realities as we now know them to be and to have been, but in even greater degree on what men imagined in regard to them." [12]

Another British geographer, the late K. G. T. Clark, extended this distinction between image and environmental reality to other features of the milieu, and attempted to bring its social implications into sharper focus: "An African with no experience of the world outside his native forest, transported by magic carpet to one of our [British brick] houses, would perceive what we also perceive, a prevailingly red object of certain shape. But because his previous experience vastly differs from ours, it is impossible he should perceive it as a house. Yet in physico-chemical terms the house is the same whoever looks at it. In our two perceptions there is something in common, the objective element, and something different, the subjective element. Human geographers, and others who study phenomena embracing human action and its results, are up against complications due to the fact that the reaction of man to a given physical background is apt to be strongly colored by this subjective element in his apprehension of that background. The way we have . . .

[12] H. J. Mackinder, *Democratic Ideals and Reality*, Holt, 1919; reprinted in 1942, pp. 28, 30. Mackinder dwelt on this theme on many occasions. See, for example, his essay on "The Physical Basis of Political Geography," in *Scottish Geographical Magazine*, 1890, v. 6, pp. 78*ff*; also *Britain and the British Seas*, London, 1902, ch. 1; and *Distant Lands*, London, 1910, pp. 115, 117, 126.

been shaped in the past influences the reactions of the present." [13]

A third British geographer, William Kirk, has brought the viewpoint of *Gestalt* psychological theory to bear on this problem. Kirk portrays his model by the following diagram:

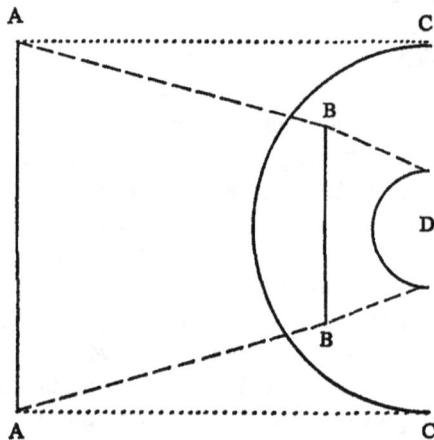

In expounding his hypothesis, he says: "If *A* represents the physical environment, including both the physical and cultural landscapes, and *C* represents the physical human group or individual present in this environment, the physical state of *C* will depend in part on the character of *A*, but any action of *C* in this environment will

[13] K. G. T. Clark, "Certain Underpinnings of Our Arguments in Human Geography," in *Transactions and Papers*, Institute of British Geographers, 1950, No. 16, pp. 15, 20. This subject has been carefully and thoroughly investigated by David Lowenthal of the American Geographical Society, and the results of his research published in "Geography, Experience, and Imagination: Towards a Geographical Epistemology," in *Annals*, Association of American Geographers, 1961, v. 51, pp. 241ff. This essay is valuable not only for its own substantive content, but also for the remarkably extensive bibliographical notes.

COGNITIVE ASPECT

commence in the relief of stresses in an internal environment *B* [what we call the psycho-milieu] which are as
much the product of the group culture *D* as the act of
observation of the physical environment. This internal
[that is, psychological] environment we may call the
'behavioral environment' and in this environment the gap
is closed between Mind and Nature."

   In order to explain satisfactorily the past actions of
"human groups in relation to environment," Kirk contends that it is necessary to "reconstruct the environment
not only as it was at various dates but as it was observed
and thought to be, for it is in this behavioral [that is,
psychological] environment that physical features acquire values and potentialities which attract or repel human action. Certain features may entirely change in significance in different behavioral environments. A piece
of ground of little value in the behavioral environment
of one group may become suddenly desirable in that of another group." [14]

   Mackinder, Clarke, Kirk, and others who might be
cited have emphasized the psychological response that
gives meaning to what is perceived. Psychologists also
emphasize that perception itself is selective. An individual never perceives everything that is present in the milieu.
We have previously called attention to the possible importance of what is not perceived. Unperceived environmental factors may be strategic in the execution of decisions, as was the case in the American debacle at Pearl

[14] William Kirk, "Historical Geography and the Concept of the
Behavioral Environment," in *Indian Geographical Journal*, Silver
Jubilee Volume, 1951, pp. 152, 160. A similar point has been made
by American geographers. See, for example, P. E. James *et al.*,
American Geography: Inventory and Prospect, Syracuse University
Press, 1954, p. 13; also Derwent Whittlesey, "The Horizon of
Geography," in *Annals*, Association of American Geographers,
1945, v. 35, pp. 1*ff*.

Harbor, in our illustrative example of the man who tumbled headlong into the unperceived open manhole, and in other instances cited in the preceding chapters. But the selectivity of perception is also relevant in the context of behavioral analysis: that is to say, in the explanation or prediction of decisions and the psychological antecedents of decisions, as well as in explanation or prediction of the operational results of decisions.

The psychologist R. G. Barker sums up this behavioral relevance as follows: ". . . it is generally agreed by students of perception and learning that the ecological environment [that is, the operational milieu] does not demand behavior, but that it is, rather, permissive, supportive, or resistive. It is true that a language is often used that implies at least a triggering function for the ecological environment: events in the environment are said to stimulate, to evoke, to instigate behavior. And the fact that experiments are by design usually conducted within environments that are, indeed, stimulating gives support to the language used. However, the fine print of psychological theory always, so far as I have been able to determine, makes the intrapersonal sector of the [E-E] arc [that is, environment to organism to environment] the arbiter of what will be received as stimuli [by the environed individual], and how it will be coded and programmed in the intrapersonal sector before it emerges as output. The simple fact is that to function as a stimulus, an environmental variable must be received by the organism." [15]

In addition to environmental factors that a given individual is incapable of perceiving (for example, the open manhole in the pitch-dark street), many conditions may affect one's receptivity to particular potential stimuli. Of-

[15] R. G. Barker, "On the Nature of the Environment," in *Journal of Social Issues*, 1963, v. 19, no. 4, pp. 17, 20-21.

ficers upon the bridge are likely to be acutely alert to changes of weather that may not be noticed by most passengers in a ship at sea. An individual arrested and dragged off to jail is likely to be more aware of the police than someone walking along the street preoccupied with what to give his children for Christmas.

To put the matter more generally, habituation to values, taboos, working rules, and other norms prevailing within a social group—government agency, political community, or the like—may condition individuals to be more alert and responsive to certain features of the milieu than to others. An individual's role and the norms implicit in it may likewise condition the kinds of responses he makes to what he perceives. In any sector of human affairs one may discern regularities in perceptions and responses. Such regularities provide data for the behavioral models described in the preceding chapter. But such models, it must be remembered, describe only behavior on the average, behavior that is more or less typical, more or less normally expectable in the milieu in question. In any specific instance, the behavior of an individual may or may not conform to the norm. The odds for conformity may be strong, but in the final test it is the individual, not his milieu, that determines what will be perceived and how it will be reacted to.

Importance of this distinction between the individual's psycho-milieu to which his self-conscious behavior is related, and the operational milieu in which his decisions are executed, has long been recognized, though often disregarded. It was the central concept of Walter Lippmann's pioneering book on public opinion, published in the early 1920's. The title of the opening chapter set the frame of discussion: "The World Outside and the Pictures in Our Heads." Political behavior (Lippmann could just as well

have said all self-conscious human behavior) is characterized as a response to a "pseudo-environment" consist-
ing of the individual's perceptions and interpretations of
his milieu. "The way in which the world is imagined determines at any particular moment what men will do. It
does not determine what they will achieve. It determines
their efforts, their feelings, their hopes, not their accomplishments and results." [16]

The concept of psycho-milieu (though not designated by
this term) became the point of departure in a ground-
breaking project carried out, in the early 1950's by R. C.
Snyder and two associates, H. W. Bruck and Burton Sapin. In a long essay entitled "Decision-Making as an Approach to the Study of International Politics," [17] the thesis
was advanced and skillfully argued that the milieu that
matters (which those authors call the "setting") is the
milieu as perceived and reacted to by the state's official
agents, called the "decision-makers."

On this issue Snyder and his associates are very explicit:
"It should be perfectly clear that, as far as the actors in
the [decisional] system are concerned, information that is
not in use or is not recognized as information does not
exist at all. Files, intelligence reports, research and all the
paraphernalia of modern administration might just as well
not exist at all if they are not used. Moreover, a particular message may have no meaning in an actor's schema
of the external world and may consequently be disre-

[16] Walter Lippmann, *Public Opinion*, Macmillan, 1922, pp. 3,
25-26.
[17] This essay was published in a limited edition in 1954 by the
now defunct Organizational Behavior Project of Princeton University. It was widely and sometimes harshly reviewed, and has exerted
a continuing influence on the development of theory in the field of
international politics. The essay was reprinted, without revision, in
Snyder, Brook, and Sapin, *Foreign Policy Decision Making*, Free
Press, 1962, pp. 14-185.

garded. Here again it is of the utmost importance for the student to investigate the nature of the world of the decision-maker."

This thesis is reiterated again and again, in such sentences as: "Relevance of particular factors and conditions *in general* and *in particular situations* will depend on the attitudes, perceptions, judgments, and purposes of State-X's decision-makers, that is, on how they react to various stimuli."

The authors do recognize, we hasten to add, that the milieu may also be relevant to the study of international politics in ways other than via the cognition of the official agents of the state. On this issue they say: "It should be noted that our conception of setting [that is, the cognized factors of the milieu which the decision-maker regards as relevant to his purposes] does *not* exclude certain so-called environmental limitations such as the state of technology . . . which *may* limit the achievement of objectives or which *may* otherwise become part of the conditions of action *irrespective* of *whether* and *how* the decision-makers perceive them."

However, read in context, the sentence just quoted evokes doubt as to whether Snyder and his colleagues really attached much importance to uncognized limitations present in the decision-maker's milieu—for their text continues: "However—and this is important—this [that is, their recognition of possible relevance of uncognized or disregarded environing conditions and events] does not in our scheme imply the substitution of an omniscient observer's judgment for that of the decision-maker. Setting is an analytical device to suggest certain enduring kinds of relevances and to limit the number of non-governmental factors with which the student of international politics must be concerned. The external setting is constantly

· 135 ·

changing and will be composed of *what the decision-makers decide is important"* (italics as in original).[18]

The reference to "omniscient observer" is to the familiar analytic device sometimes employed to sharpen the distinction between the milieu as perceived and reacted to by a specified individual, and the milieu in its total relation to that individual as this would appear to an observer who sees all and knows all. Of course, as previously emphasized, no observer is actually omniscient; but the construct of hypothetical omniscient observer helps to emphasize the limitations of a particular individual's own knowledge of his milieu. This device also helps to emphasize the different perspective and, in some instances, the quite different knowledge which a particular *actual* observer may bring to bear on a specified actor's *total* relations to the milieu in which he is operating.

Whether one finds the device of hypothetical omniscient observer useful or not may depend on various considerations; but it is *methodologically impossible* to dispense with the viewpoint of *some* observer. Either one has to ignore the environing factors that are unperceived or disregarded by the individual or group under consideration, or else one must introduce the outside observer who analyzes environmental limitations that affect the operational results of decisions *irrespective of whether or how* these are perceived and reacted to in the process of decision-making.

Moreover, even if one were to concentrate exclusively on the "universe" of the decision-maker, he could not thereby get rid of the observer. Except for the situation in which a person analyzes his *own* perceptions, there is necessarily some observer on the scene—else there would be no report and no analysis of the behavior. "Probing

[18] *Ibid.*, pp. 67, 134.

the minds of decision-makers in terms of their official behavior," a concept introduced early in the Snyder scheme,
carries inescapably a built-in outside observer who does
the "probing." In the final analysis, reconstruction of the
"world of the decision-maker," as well as the identification and evaluation of noncognitive relations between decision-maker and his milieu, assumes the existence of
someone to perform the analytical operations involved.

Not infrequently—probably usually in complex undertakings characteristic of foreign affairs—the psycho-milieu
of the individual or group initiating a course of action
includes predictive assumptions as to the future state of
the milieu. The British decision to reoccupy the Suez
Canal in October 1956 illustrates this complicating feature. Suppose, for the purpose of illustration, that the decision to intervene was predicated on some such estimate
as follows: that the operation could be executed quickly;
that the Egyptians could neither resist nor block the canal;
that other Arab peoples would not disrupt production and
delivery of oil to Europe contrary to their manifest economic interest; that the Soviet government would keep its
hands off; that the United States and Commonwealth
governments would accept a *fait accompli;* that the United
Nations could offer no serious obstacle; and that public
opposition in Britain would collapse as soon as British
forces were re-established in the canal zone.

In the Suez case, as in all complex situations, the operational milieu included many easily ascertainable conditions. But latent in that milieu were potential human responses to the decisions under consideration. Those responses, when they did occur, became part of the operational milieu in which the decision to intervene was executed. That they did not exist prior to the decision added
a complicating element of uncertainty to the decision-
maker's problem. But such uncertainty does not invalidate

the thesis that environmental factors can become related to policy decisions only as they are perceived and taken into account in the decision-making process. The Suez example rather emphasizes that the decision-maker's estimate of the situation may frequently (perhaps nearly always) have to include not merely phenomena existent prior to the decisions but also his own predictions as to how the milieu will change as the decision is carried into execution.

This aspect of the Suez example directs attention to an important limitation of cognitive behavioral research. An analyst might reconstruct (from verbal or other evidence) the *expectations* (that is, the predictions) of Prime Minister Eden and his colleagues regarding changes that were likely to occur in the situation (milieu) as their course of action proceeded. But such a reconstruction would not constitute prediction on the part of the analyst himself. Moreover, one cannot investigate empirically a decision or any other event that has not occurred. So-called "probing the minds" of decision-makers is a historical, not a predictive, mode of analysis.

Some features of the milieu, in any given problem, may remain relatively unchanged during shorter or longer periods of time. Other features may change radically within the time-span of the problem in hand. There is also likely to be some degree of constancy in the behavioral patterns of particular persons and groups. But all predictions of choices and decisions involve in some degree, usually in major degree, the substitution of assumptions in place of evidence, with respect both to the milieu and to the environed individual's responses thereto.

Even in historical cases, the cognitive approach requires access to specific verbal or other data. When such data is unreliable, scanty, or lacking altogether, one has no recourse but to fall back on general models derived from assumptions as to what was normally expectable behavior in the milieu in question.

Finally, neither probabilistic models of behavior nor specific data on the behavior of particular individuals, nor both together, ever cover the full spectrum of man-milieu relationships. *No more than possibilism do the behavioral approaches provide a comprehensive frame of reference.* To the behavioral thesis that it is the "idea formed of the environment which matters as much as the brute fact," one might counter, in the idiom of O. H. K. Spate, that people cannot use a raw material that does not exist, no matter what idea they form about it.[19]

Within these limitations the cognitive approach is a valuable tool. It provides a corrective check on loose generalities about what Russians or Chinese or others "are like." Efforts to reconstruct the psychological environment of particular decision-makers also (as previously emphasized) adds to the inventory of data from which better general models may be derived. In this way, the cognitive approach contributes *indirectly* to prediction as well as to historical explanation. This complementarity is important and should be clearly understood.[20]

As previously noted, investigation of cognitive environmental relationships may be conducted with a minimum of formal apparatus. That is the way narrative history is usually written. Or one can utilize a formal analytical scheme such as the one proposed by Snyder and his asso-

[19] Commenting on this issue, Egon Brunswik says: "The 'field' within which Lewin is able to predict, in the strict sense of the word, is the person in his life space. But the life space is not to be confused with geographic environment of physical stimuli, nor with actually achieved results in the environment." "The Probability Point of View," in *Psychological Theory,* edited by M. H. Marx, Macmillan, 1951, p. 197.

[20] This complementarity thesis is argued at length in the paper by Brunswik, cited just above.

ciates. In either case, the central thesis is the same: *Moods, attitudes, values, preferences, choices, decisions, projects and undertakings are relatable to the milieu through the perceptions and other psychological processes of the environed individual*—AND IN NO OTHER WAY! [21]

Before leaving this subject, it would be well to note that one can make too much of discongruities between psychological image and environmental reality. The fact that the human species has survived (thus far) suggests that there must be considerable congruity between the milieu as it actually is and as most people conceive it to be. One might conclude from the histories of technology and social institutions (which are histories of manipulation as well as observation of the milieu) that the degree of congruity tends on the whole to increase through time. In particular, one might conclude that individuals with similar backgrounds tend in the main to apperceive rather similarly the milieu which encompasses them. Indeed, all explanations and predictions of human behavior on the basis of general assumptions regarding motivation and purpose, environmental knowledge, decision-making, etc. (as discussed in the preceding chapter), rest upon the still more basic premise, generally confirmed by experience, that approximate congruity is more typical than radical discongruity within the same nation, class, or other social grouping.

At the same time, because of significant individual var-

[21] Throughout this chapter we have deliberately bypassed certain areas of uncertainty and dispute in psychological theory; in particular, hypotheses as to what takes place between stimulus and response in the so-called "black box" of the human mind. We have bypassed this issue because it is both controversial and also only marginal to the frame in which our own discussion is placed. On the range of behavioral theories, see C. E. Osgood, "Behavior Theory and the Social Sciences," in *Approaches to the Study of Politics*, edited by Roland Young, Northwestern University Press, 1958, pp. 217*ff*.

iations in perception and interpretation of the milieu, even within relatively homogeneous social groups, general behavioral models tend to be less sharp tools than one would desire. Thus one returns to the widely felt need, in the analysis of choices and decisions, as distinguished from the operational results of given decisions, for more empirical evidence from which to reconstruct the universe of specific individuals and groups, and thereby, and indirectly, to accumulate larger inventories of data from which to construct more reliable general models.

8

MAN-MILIEU RELATIONSHIPS RECON-
SIDERED IN THE LIGHT OF MORE
GENERAL THEORIES OF EXPLANATION

DURING THE 1950's a sequence of papers by British
scholars gave a new turn to the discussion of man-milieu
relationship doctrines. First in this sequence was an address by K. G. T. Clark, presented in 1950 to the Institute of British Geographers. Clark posed verbal and logical difficulties inherent in the conventional modes of
phrasing man-milieu relationships.[1] This paper drew a
reply from A. F. Martin of the School of Geography at
Oxford. On philosophical and logical grounds, Martin
argued determinism to be the only doctrine compatible
with the notion of causality and the orderly operation of
causal laws.[2]

Martin's paper in turn evoked two more. One of these,
a collaborative product by a philosopher, A. C. Montefiore, and a geographer-sociologist, W. M. Williams, proposed clarifying man-milieu relationships by restating
them in terms of more general explanation theory.[3] In
the fourth paper, the geographer Emrys Jones contended
that Martin had confused the idea of causality as understood and applied in physical science, with a metaphysical

---

[1] K. G. T. Clark, "Certain Underpinnings of Our Arguments in
Human Geography," in *Transactions and Papers,* Institute of British Geographers, 1950, no. 16, pp. 15-21.

[2] A. F. Martin, "The Necessity for Determinism," in *ibid.,* 1951,
no. 17, pp. 1-11.

[3] A. C. Montefiore and W. M. Williams, "Determinism and Possibilism," in *Geographical Studies,* 1955, v. 2, pp. 1*ff.*

concept of ultimate cause; and that explanatory hypotheses in social science, as in physical science, are simply empirical generalizations expressing average expectable regularities.[4]

Taken together, these four essays constitute a significant episode in the evolution of thinking about man-milieu relationships. All four represent efforts to break away from the hackneyed disputation that had long enveloped this subject. Hypotheses about man-milieu relationships all reflect attempts to explain human undertakings and accomplishments. As such they constitute an aspect of explanation in general. There is an important literature on the nature of scientific and historical explanations. Students of geography and of politics appear to have given remarkably little attention to this literature. Yet much of it is definitely relevant. All of the above papers, but the one by Montefiore and Williams in particular, direct attention to the possibility of sharpening the discussion of man-milieu relationships by translating environmental doctrines into the vocabulary of more general theories of explanation.[5]

What is involved in "explaining" a past event or com-

[4] Emrys Jones, "Cause and Effect in Human Geography," in *Annals*, Association of American Geographers, 1956, v. 46, pp. 369-77.

[5] There is a fair sampling of the literature of explanation theory in three anthologies: *Theories of History*, edited by Patrick Gardiner, Free Press, 1959; *Readings in Philosophical Analysis*, edited by Herbert Feigl and Wilfrid Sellars, Appleton-Century-Crofts, 1949, esp. pp. 459-544; *Readings in the Philosophy of Science*, edited by Herbert Feigl and May Brodbeck, Appleton-Century-Crofts, 1953, esp. pp. 663-754. Some additional items are cited in the following pages. Our attention was first drawn to this literature by Messrs. Montefiore and Williams, whose paper "Determinism and Possibilism" is cited above. We have also derived benefit from conversations with our colleague Professor C. G. Hempel (of the Princeton Department of Philosophy), who read and criticized this and the following chapter in particular.

plex state of affairs? This question has been asked by many, and answered in many different ways. A recent review of explanations in history and the social sciences identifies nine more or less distinct meanings of the term *explanation:*

(1) to clarify a concept or a proposition by restating it in different words or other symbols;

(2) to demonstrate the logical steps leading to a particular conclusion;

(3) to give "a description or an outline of a temporal sequence of events" that supplies an acceptable "answer to a puzzle-question about the origin or development" of an event or state of affairs;

(4) to identify the "intentions" of the person whose actions are to be explained;

(5) to identify the "reasons" for an action, whether these are consistent or not with the "intentions" of the actor;

(6) to identify the behavioral "tendency" or "disposition" reflected in a person's actions;

(7) to identify the "functions" performed by a person or an institution;

(8) to identify a "law," that is, an observed empirical regularity, of which the event or state of affairs to be explained is a particular instance;

(9) to interpret a discrete event or state of affairs by reference to a relevant deductive theory.[6]

Some of these modes of explanation are more relational, and hence more directly relevant, than the others to the issues with which we are here concerned. In particular, types (4), (5), and (6) should cast light on the problem of relating environmental factors to choices and decisions; and types (8) and (9), to the operational results of de-

[6] Robert Brown, *Explanation in Social Science,* Aldine, 1963, esp. chs. 4-11.

cisions. Indeed, much of the discussion of explanation in history and the social sciences stems directly from a paper first published in 1942 by the philosopher C. G. Hempel, on "The Function of General Laws [as per type (8)] in History." [7]

Hempel's central thesis is that explanations of social events and states of affairs are essentially similar to explanations of nonhuman phenomena. In both types, he contends, phenomena are explained by the logical application of universal hypotheses, or "covering laws," derived by generalization of observed regularities.

Such a universal hypothesis, or law, states that "in every case where an event of a specified kind C occurs at a certain place and time, an event of a specified kind E will occur at a place and time which is related in a specified manner to the place and time of the occurrence of the first event." This rule is often expressed in such abbreviated formulas as: "where C, there E"; "the more of C, the more of E"; "in the absence of C, no E"; etc.

In logical terms, still quoting from Hempel, this mode of explanation consists of:

"(1) a set of statements asserting the occurrence of certain events $C_i \ldots C_n$, at certain times and places,

(2) a set of universal hypotheses, such that—

(a) the statements of both groups are reasonably well confirmed by empirical evidence,

(b) from the two groups of statements the sentence asserting the occurrence of event E can be logically deduced."

[7] Hempel's paper first appeared in the *Journal of Philosophy*, 1942, v. 39, pp. 35*ff*. It has since been reprinted in two of the anthologies cited above: *Theories of History*, pp. 344*ff*; and *Readings in Philosophical Analysis*, pp. 459*ff*.

This procedure presents difficulty when applied to human affairs. Hempel illustrates this difficulty by an explanatory statement regarding the migration of farmers from the Middle West to California in the 1930's. The statement says that "the Dust Bowl farmers" migrated "because continued drought and sandstorms render[ed] their existence increasingly precarious, and because California seem[ed] to them to offer so much better living conditions." This explanatory statement, Hempel says, "rests on some such universal hypothesis as that populations will migrate to regions which offer better living conditions." But he stresses the difficulty of stating this hypothesis "in the form of a general law which is reasonably well confirmed by all the relevant evidence available." He adds that "analogous remarks apply to all historical explanations in terms of class struggle, economic or geographic conditions, vested interests of certain groups, tendency to conspicuous consumption, etc.: All of them rest on the assumption of universal hypotheses which connect certain characteristics of individual or group life with others; but in many cases, the content of the hypotheses which are tacitly assumed in a given explanation can be reconstructed only quite approximately." In view of this difficulty, historical explanations are often, perhaps nearly always, derived from "probability hypotheses" rather than "deterministic" laws. Such an explanation, "if fully and explicitly formulated . . . would state certain initial conditions, and certain probability hypotheses, such that the occurrence of the event to be explained is made probable by the initial conditions in view of the probability hypotheses." [8]

[8] Hempel's thesis and supporting argument have stimulated a continuing controversy among philosophers of history. We can bypass most of this controversy, since it is marginal, in the main, to our discussion of man-milieu relationship theories. For a sum-

EXPLANATION

One way to bring general explanatory hypotheses to bear on human endeavors and achievements is through the concepts of necessary and sufficient conditions. If we designate as *E* the historical event or state of affairs to be explained, a necessary condition of *E* may be defined as an event or other phenomenon, in the absence of which *E* could not have occurred. Alternatively, a necessary condition may be defined as a phenomenon, the absence of which would have justified antecedent prediction that *E* would not occur. Sometimes, a probabilistic overtone enters via such a phrase as ". . . in the absence of which *E* could *hardly* have occurred." A sufficient condition may be defined as an event or other phenomenon, the occurrence of which would have justified antecedent prediction that *E* would occur.[9]

How does one identify the necessary and sufficient conditions of a given historical *E*? The answer is simple in principle: by logical application of relevant general explanatory hypotheses, as described by Hempel and others. From such hypotheses one identifies and deduces the significance of antecedent (sometimes concomitant) conditions to the given *E* for which the explanation is sought. In practice, this operation may prove extremely difficult. This is so (in the words of the philosopher Ernest Nagel) "since the full circumstances are quite often complex and numerous and are usually not known," and since "in this area of inquiry . . . we do not possess at present a

mary, in which many of the participants in this debate are cited, see R. H. Weingartner, "The Quarrel About Historical Explanation," in *Journal of Philosophy*, 1961, v. 58, pp. 29ff. In 1962, Hempel re-examined the issues in a paper entitled "Explanation in Science and in History," ch. 1 of *Frontiers of Science and Philosophy*, edited by R. G. Colodny, University of Pittsburgh Press.

[9] For a discussion of necessary and sufficient conditions in the specific context of environmental theory, see Montefiore and Williams, "Determinism and Possibilism" (cited above), pp. 5ff.

generally accepted, explicitly formulated, and fully comprehensive schema for weighing the evidence for any arbitrarily given hypothesis. . . ." Fortunately, Nagel concludes, "though the range of possible disagreement concerning the force of evidence for a given statement is theoretically limitless, there is substantial agreement among men experienced in relevant matters on the relative probabilities to be assigned to many hypotheses." [10]

Where do these general explanatory hypotheses come from, from which one deduces the necessary and/or sufficient conditions of a given E? They are not discovered. Such hypotheses—or covering laws, as they are also called—do not exist independently in Nature. They are *invented*. They are products of someone's creative imagination. Explanatory hypotheses appear in many forms—ranging all the way from the precise equations of the physical sciences, to the generally more imprecise, often implicit, rules "by which we guide our conduct and try to insure that it will lead to a known future" in the day-to-day business of carrying on our affairs in a milieu composed of our fellowmen and the nonhuman factors of environment. [11]

Explanatory hypotheses are generalized statements of relationships between phenomena. In model form, as previously indicated, they are often expressed by such formulas as: "Where C, there E," or, "the more of C, the more of E"; or "in the absence of C, no E." Such a formula

[10] Ernest Nagel, "The Logic of Historical Analysis," reprinted in Feigl and Brodbeck, *Readings in the Philosophy of Science*, pp. 688, 697, 700. There are numerous dissenters from this conception of historical explanation, who contend that identification of necessary and/or sufficient conditions is by no means all that is involved. See, for example, W. B. Gallie, "Explanations in History and the Genetic Sciences," in *Mind, A Quarterly Journal of Psychology and Philosophy*, 1955, v. 64, pp. 160ff.

[11] Jacob Bronowski, *The Common Sense of Science*, Harvard University Press, 1953, p. 105.

EXPLANATION

may express an observed regularity in the phenomena
under consideration, in which case it is also called an
"empirical generalization" or an "inductive hypothesis."
Or the formula may state a purely hypothetical relationship, such as: "if C were so-and-so, then E would be
such-and-such." Such formulas, derived from empirical
regularities, observed or hypothesized, differ from theories
derived from concepts of "ideal" types which have no
possible counterpart in the "real world": for example,
the concept of "economic man" in pure economic theory.[12]

The astrophysicist J. Q. Stewart has given an interesting account of hypothesis-building, which involves both
inductive generalization and deductive theorizing. In connection with certain research on which he was engaged
during World War II, Stewart was impressed by evi-
dences of the apparent pull or attraction or simply effect
on human activities that cities exhibit beyond their geographic boundaries. Suburbs, filling stations, shopping
centers, motels, restaurants, highway and railway grids,
and many other social structures at varying distances all
bear evidence of the city's presence. Could one formulate
a general formula (law, hypothesis) that would express
these relationships? Being a physical scientist, he naturally
turned to that source for possibly fruitful analogies.

"Whatever the motives that influence individual persons [Stewart reasoned], the *positions* of people in space
at any instant, and their *motions* from one point to another, come into the purview of physics, and only indirectly into that of psychology." He found the familiar
"dot map," designed to show densities of population over
a geographic area, to be useful but inadequate, because
"the sociological influences of 100,000 people are not

[12] Empirical generalizations and deductive theories are examined
from the standpoint of social analysis, in Brown, *Explanation in
Social Science*, chs. 10-11.

· 149 ·

confined to the immediate neighborhood of the city blocks where they live. . . . Common sense indicates that the influence of many people is more than the influence of a few, and that their influence at a distance is less than near at hand."

This suggested an analogy from the physical law of electrostatic potential. Would that rule hold for social entities in space? From this analogy, Stewart derived the concept of "potentials of population," and the general explanatory hypothesis that the influence of an aggregate of people is "proportional" to their number, "divided by their distance away from the point where their influence is measured." [13]

He tried out the rule on various kinds of activities and layouts. It appeared to fit rather well. He did not claim then, or later, that observation would invariably confirm the rule, but simply that it appeared to hold on the average with sufficient regularity to provide a basis for predicting a varied assortment of influences, or effects, which Stewart, and later the geographer William Warntz, have investigated.[14]

[13] J. Q. Stewart, *Coasts, Waves and Weather*, Ginn, 1945, pp. 162ff.

[14] See J. Q. Stewart and W. Warntz, "Macrogeography and Social Science," in *Geographical Review*, 1958, v. 48, pp. 167ff; Stewart and Warntz, "Physics of Population Distribution," in *Journal of Regional Science*, 1958, v. 1, pp. 99ff; Warntz, "Measuring Spatial Associations with Special Consideration of the Case of Market Orientation of Production," in *Journal of the American Statistical Association*, 1956, v. 51, pp. 597ff; "Number of People and Distance as Basic Dimensions for Behavioral Science," Northwestern University Conference on Ecological and Behavioral Models, Evanston, June 1958; "Geography at Mid-Twentieth Century," in *World Politics*, 1959, v. 11, pp. 442ff; "Social Physics: A Macrogeographer Takes a Hard Look at College Enrollments," in *Princeton Alumni Weekly*, September 18, 1959; "A New Map of the Surface of Population Potentials for the United States, 1960," in *Geographical Review*, 1964, v. 54, pp. 170ff.

EXPLANATION

The Stewart-Warntz operations, and others of a similar kind, have evoked at least two sorts of objections. The first relates to the requirements of a "satisfactory" or "acceptable" explanation. The second relates to the utility of an explanatory hypothesis that holds only part of the time.

Regarding the first point, many will ask: *Why* does the rule hold to the degree that it appears to? One possible answer is simply to restate the rule. In this instance such an answer would say: the rule holds because the influence of an aggregate of people is observed to be proportional . . . , etc. Another possible answer is the one given by the geographer Emrys Jones, who says that this sort of "why" question "hardly ever arises in science. It is pushed back into the realm of metaphysics" and generally left there. "The most pressing question in science is 'how.' Relationships can be explained on this basis without taking the problem further than its immediate context"—and that, it may be noted, is precisely where Stewart and Warntz have left it.[15]

One does not have to leave the issue there, however. The question that Jones says most scientists leave to the metaphysicians can also be tackled empirically at the micro-level. Suppose the phenomena in question are the commuting patterns of people living at varying distances from New York and Philadelphia. Suppose it is ascertained that more people commute longer distances to New York than to Philadelphia, and further that Stewart's population-distance rule expresses the observed pattern rather closely. If one desires a more specific explanation, he must go to a more specific level of investigation. One might interview a sample of commuters. Or if one had

[15] Emrys Jones, "Cause and Effect in Human Geography," in *Annals*, Association of American Geographers, 1956, v. 46, pp. 369, 373-74.

sufficient resources, he might interrogate every one of them. Or if he had the staff and enough moral suasion or authority, he might subject some or all to psychoanalysis.

From such procedures the investigator might derive at least two kinds of knowledge: (1) data for probabilistic behavioral hypotheses that account, on the average, for the psychic motivations underlying the events that are expressed (without regard to volition) in the population-distance rule; and (2) explanatory accounts of the particular motivations and decisions of particular individuals. Probabilistic behavioral hypotheses so derived can be used to add a volitional dimension to the population-distance rule, expressible in some such sentence as: the rule holds because. . . . Or such probabilistic hypotheses can be used to supplement investigation designed to reconstruct the psychic behavior of particular individuals. In such research, it should be noted, one has shifted definitely from the *macro*-level of explanation in terms of average expectable behavior, to the *micro*-level of explanation of the specific behavior of particular individuals.

Not all "why" questions, it should be noted, can be answered to everyone's satisfaction. At any given stage in the development of any science or discipline, there are always observed regularities or patterns that simply have to be taken for granted, since no satisfactory explanatory hypotheses to account for them have yet been invented. It should also be noted that "why" questions can be pushed back to ultimate philosophical postures. At that level one may get such answers as: a given rule holds because it represents "the inscrutable will of God," or because "the Universe is a machine," or because things just happen to work that way, etc. For people who are

EXPLANATION

not too preoccupied with "ultimate causes," the simple knowledge that a given hypothesis holds within some more or less ascertainable margin of error may be sufficient for most purposes.

The notion of error, or exceptions to the rule, bring us to the second question: What use is a rule that holds only part of the time? Those who profess to believe in a deterministic universe are likely to answer that an explanatory law or hypothesis is invalidated by a single instance in which events fail to conform to the law. In the words of the Oxford geographer A. F. Martin: "We can scarcely think of the universe except in terms of causation. Now if we are to believe at all in cause and effect, we must believe in their absolute rigorousness. There can be no exceptions. The same cause, if it really is identical and not merely similar, must always be followed by the same effect, without any room for doubt or choice. Similarly every phenomenon must have its cause; there can be nothing uncaused." [16]

This philosophical posture can be neither confirmed nor refuted. But one can *prefer* a different posture; and such is the purport of Emrys Jones's rejoinder to Martin: "If the actions of a large number of human beings follow a pattern, however variable the human motivations, then generalizations or broad principles can be drawn up. But however broad the generalization, it might fail in strict application to any single phenomenon. Any pattern which emerges does so as the statistical mean of the behavior of a mass of human individuals, and any generalizations which the human geographer [or any other analyst of human affairs] might find useful must be based on this behavior. The issue is often confused when the regularity

[16] A. F. Martin, "The Necessity for Determinism," in *Transactions and Papers,* Institute of British Geographers, 1951, No. 17, pp. 1, 5-6.

of certain sequences which could be stated as a generalization is related to determinism." [17]

The posture that one takes on this issue will have intellectual consequences—and frequently moral and civic consequences as well. A disposition towards determinism may be implicit in a felt need for an orderly social as well as physical universe governed by tight "covering laws," causal premises that are universally "true," and pursuit of "why" questions to ultimate philosophical predicates. If one finds acceptable a less tidy, probabilistic view of the universe, this is likely to be reflected in satisfaction wih explanatory premises that events confirm on the average but with numerous exceptions, and philosophical acceptance of the uncertainty that pervades most human affairs.

In practice, most people's behavior appears to include some mixture of these antithetical postures. Their daily speech is filled with dogmatic causal statements: for example A's headache was caused by eyestrain; B's car was wrecked because a tire blew out; C became ill from eating poison mushrooms; etc. On the other hand, nonverbal behavior, rather more than habits of speaking, suggest that the same people usually make the countless unrecorded decisions of daily living in accord with probabilistic expectations. It is notorious, for example, that car drivers occasionally run through an intersection against a red signal. This knowledge, however, does not deter most pedestrians from crossing the street. In stepping from the curb they are acting on the assumption that adverse traffic normally observes the rules.

Comparable inconsistency may also be evident in more formal behavior. For example, some theorists of political systems offer strongly deterministic models, often with ex-

[17] Jones, "Cause and Effect in Human Geography," p. 373.

plicit analogies to machines and organisms, and the accompanying implication that the system is not under the volitional control of its constituents. Yet, in other contexts, the same theorists may behave as if genuinely convinced that their civic activities really can significantly affect public policies—and hence the operation of the system as a whole.

The task of explaining a historical event or state of affairs (which we shall continue to designate E) may be conceived in at least two ways: (1) why did E occur? (2) how was it possible for E to occur? Explanation theorists have divided on the issue of whether an explanation, in order to be satisfactory, must answer the "why" question as well as the "how possible" question, and whether the "why" question should be construed as "why necessarily" or simply "why possibly." Positions taken on these issues are generally associated with the opposing postures, reviewed above, as to the need for explanatory hypotheses which are, or are not, invariably confirmed by events.

If the "why" question is construed as "why necessarily," it involves locating a set of conditions that are individually necessary and jointly sufficient to account for the occurrence of E. Some of the most persistent efforts to do this are represented in the various environmentalistic interpretations of history: interpretations in which the necessary and sufficient conditions are identified as the grouping and configuration of lands and seas, or the geographical distribution of fertility and/or mineral resources, or spatial and temporal variations of climate, or distributions of population in space and through time, and various other sets of environmental factors. The strict environmental determinist contends that the history that did occur was the only history that could have occurred, and that one could have predicted its inevitable occurrence

by the distribution in space and through time of the set
of environmental factors hypothesized to be the individually necessary and jointly sufficient conditions of that history.[18]

Since human history, unlike controlled experiments
in the laboratory, cannot be repeated, and since collateral
conditions cannot be held constant, there is no conclusive
way either to confirm or to refute deterministic interpretations of history as a whole. The same holds for deterministic explanations of particular historical events and
states of affairs. Nevertheless, deterministic overtones
creep into historical discourse under such verbalisms as
"*the* cause," "the *real* cause," or "the *true* cause."

Some philosophers of history insist that this position
is precisely where one is likely to be taken by efforts to
formulate universally valid "covering laws." Though this
contention loses much of its force when it is explicitly
recognized that most explanatory hypotheses relevant to
human affairs are probabilistic rather than deterministic,[19]
William Dray and others urge historians to concentrate
on showing how it was possible for a given *E* to have
occurred: that is, to concentrate on identifying at least

[18] In Chapter III, we reviewed several of the more familiar
environmental interpretations of history, of which perhaps the most
rigorously deterministic was the one formulated by Demolins.

[19] After re-examining the issues in the light of objections raised,
Hempel reaffirms his position as follows: "The nature of understanding, in the sense in which explanation is meant to give us an
understanding of empirical phenomena, is basically the same in all
areas of scientific inquiry; and . . . the deductive and the probabilistic model of nomological explanation accommodate vastly
more than just the explanatory arguments of, say, classical me-
chanics: in particular, they accord well also with the character of
explanations that deal with the influence of rational deliberation,
of conscious and subconscious motives, and of ideas and ideals on
the shaping of historical events." "Explanations in Science and in
History," p. 31 of *Frontiers of Science and Philosophy*, edited by
R. G. Golodny, University of Pittsburgh Press, 1962.

some of the more significant necessary conditions of E, and to leave the problem of identifying E's sufficient conditions pretty much alone.[20]

Concentration on "how possible" necessary conditions may be adequate when the task is to explain the operational outcome of a given decision or set of decisions. But answering the "how possible" question does not yield a satisfactory explanation of the decisions themselves. And decisions, it should be remembered, comprise a large part of human history. We shall return to this issue of explaining decisions in a moment.

Whether phenomena asserted to be necessary to a given E are properly so characterized is determined (as previously stated) by inference from general explanatory premises which the analyst judges to be satisfactorily confirmed, or verified, by observed events and/or consistent with other satisfactorily verified theories. Thus, if we say that the steel-moldboard plow was a necessary condition of successful cultivation of the North American prairie in the nineteenth century, this is a conclusion inferred from an explanatory hypothesis that might be expressed as follows: The physical properties of wood and iron are such that plows made of these materials do not scour clean under certain specified conditions of soil and sod, whereas plows made with steel moldboards, because of the different physical properties of steel, turn over and break up such refractory sod without fouling.

In practice, it is rarely possible to identify particular phenomena as uniquely meeting the test of "without which no E." In the example just cited, invention of the steel moldboard plow unquestionably solved a refractory technological problem, and large-scale farming of the prairie followed in due course. Does this mean that the stated

[20] See William Dray, *Laws and Explanations in History*, Oxford University Press, 1957, ch. 6.

invention was a necessary condition of the subsequent state of affairs? The answer is yes, if one means thereby that the invention rendered possible what had previously been impossible. But the answer is inconclusive if by "necessary condition" one means to assert that no alternative invention could have been followed by the same or similar operational result.

To meet this difficulty, explanation theorists have introduced the concept of "disjunctive sets"—that is, alternative sets—of necessary conditions of a given E. Since one can rarely, if ever, know that he has identified all possible sets of necessary conditions of a given E, he can ordinarily go no further than to conclude that the phenomena identified as necessary conditions of E rendered possible a state of affairs which an indefinite number of alternative sets of phenomena might likewise have rendered possible.[21]

By now it should be apparent that the concept of necessary conditions is quite similar to the concept of environmental opportunities and limitations upon which is founded the man-milieu doctrine of possibilism. But the former way of formulating the issues offers a certain advantage over the latter. The idea of necessary conditions helps to sharpen the focus of analysis by directing attention to a specific empirical problem (that is, to a state of affairs to be explained), instead of merely to a mode of conceiving man-milieu relationships. Analysis in terms of necessary conditions also emphasizes the normal plurality of antecedent or concomitant phenomena that alternatively may be significantly necessary to the occurrence of the E in question. That is to say, the idea of alternative disjunctive sets of necessary conditions bypasses the disputation over "*the* cause" of the given E. Finally, the signifi-

[21] See, for example, Montefiore and Williams, "Determinism and Possibilism," in *Geographical Studies*, 1955, v. 2, pp. 8-9.

cantly necessary conditions of E include not only the environmental factors and the features of the environed unit that rendered E possible, but also the decision, or decisions (if any) that set in motion the sequence of events from which E eventually emerged. Thus one can utilize the concept of individually necessary and jointly sufficient conditions as a sort of *analytic bridge for linking together the two aspects of man-milieu relationship represented in the initiatory decision and in the subsequent execution.*

A satisfactory explanation requires more than a mere listing of phenomena identified as necessary to the occurrence of a given E. For example, an obviously necessary condition of British command of the sea in the Napoleonic War was the existence of human beings upon the earth. But mention of that necessary condition adds nothing interesting or significant to an explanation of how it was possible for the British navy to perform certain functions generalized in the expression "command of the seas." This is so because human beings are necessary not merely to this particular $E,$ but to every E within the frame of reference which we call human history.

Various adjectives are used to distinguish from the totality of necessary conditions those which are adjudged to matter most, or to be most consequential, with reference to the problem under consideration. One such adjective is "strategic," used to emphasize a necessary condition which is adjudged by a particular analyst to be the most important or consequential to the given $E,$ or probably so. What conditions are strategic depends not only on the judgment of the analyst, but also on the level of generality at which the problem is stated. In the last example cited, the level is not human affairs in general, nor politics in general, nor military operations in general, nor seapower in general, nor British seapower in general, but British seapower during a specific period of history.

Whether a given condition is deemed to be strategic may also depend on the comparative aspect of the problem. What factors, for example, are most consequential to an explanation of the relative capacities of Britain and France to control the essential sea routes in the Napoleonic War, or to an explanation of the different levels of British achievement in that war and in earlier or later wars, or to an explanation of what could be achieved with a given effort as compared with what could be achieved with greater or lesser effort?

In explaining how a given E was possible, one may decide (depending on the nature of the problem) to break down the delineation of necessary conditions from a higher to a lower order of generality. For example, it may help to distinguish between those conditions that were necessary for E to come into existence, and those that were necessary for E to continue in existence and/or to vary in calculable ways through a given span of time. These two subcategories of necessary conditions are sometimes called "prerequisites" and "requisites" respectively. An explanation may also be enriched by distinguishing between "functions" and "structures": that is, by distinguishing between what was accomplished and how that which was accomplished was done. This distinction between functions and structures is more or less analogous to the familiar analytic distinction between ends and means.[22]

Concepts may be systematically arranged in sets of various kinds. Such a set is called a *conceptual scheme*. It can be likened to a collection of filing boxes into which one sorts elements or aspects of a state of affairs or process to be explained. A conceptual scheme, built

[22] See M. J. Levy, Jr., *The Structure of Society*, Princeton University Press, 1952, pp. 55-62.

in accordance with an ordered set of principles and relationships, is also called a *taxonomy*.

No conceptual scheme, however precise, elegant, and detailed it may be, provides a ready-made account of how it was possible for a given E to come into existence or an account of how it was possible for E to continue in existence and/or vary through some period of time. Conceptual schemes may be useful, even indispensable, in setting up and solving a problem. Such schemes may also help to generate explanatory hypotheses in the mind of the analyst. But (and this point should be obvious from what has gone before) it is the hypotheses, not the conceptual scheme, from which the analyst deduces what conditions are strategic as well as merely necessary for the occurrence and/or persistence and variation of a given historical E.

Suppose the problem is to derive general explanatory hypotheses (premises, laws) to explain the effects of various conditions of the atmosphere on human survival and behavior. From past observations and experiments in biological laboratories, one quickly establishes that atmospheric oxygen, water-vapor, and certain other chemical ingredients of the atmosphere are necessary conditions for survival of human organisms. By further observation, supplemented by controlled experiments, it can be established that human organisms respond in various describable ways to changes in atmospheric conditions. In order to derive more comprehensive and detailed knowledge of such variations in response, it may be helpful to abstract various aspects of climate and arrange them in some such conceptual scheme as follows:

(1) Atmospheric temperature
(2) Percentage of water-vapor (relative humidity)
(3) Rate of air circulation

(4) Rate of precipitation (rain, if any)
(5) Barometric pressure
(6) Other aspects

Various explanatory hypotheses can be derived from different combinations of the variables identified in the scheme. For example, observations may evoke the hypothesis that, other factors remaining constant, concomitant rises in temperature and relative humidity correlate, above a certain level, with progressive loss of mental acuity in most individuals. Numerous other hypotheses could be derived in similar manner. From these topical hypotheses one might derive more general (that is, higher-level) hypotheses about the effects of climate on human activities of many kinds. As previously emphasized, none of the hypotheses could be discovered ready-made in nature or in the conceptual apparatus employed. Each and every one would be a creative act of imagination, usually (though not necessarily) suggested or evoked by experiments or other observations. Sometimes the imagination runs ahead of observations, and thereby evokes new observations and experiments previously overlooked. For example, from knowledge of human behavior, derived from other sources, the analyst may speculate that certain combinations of temperature, humidity, and circulation are likely to be injurious to individuals suffering from, say, congestive heart disease—a speculative hypothesis that can be confirmed or disconfirmed by further experiments. Or the analyst might conclude that some other unknown element must be present in the atmosphere in order to account for observed responses—likewise a speculative hypothesis to be tested by further experiment and observation. In many sectors of knowledge it is possible to confirm hypotheses to a degree of probability that approaches certainty. In others, including most of the histories of human activities, one can do little more than apply as rigorously and explicitly as possible so-called canons of plausibility and credibility, which may in turn rest upon more or less confirmed hypotheses about human behavior and about variations and mutations of non-human phenomena.

The relation of concepts and explanatory hypotheses in the analysis and explanation of historical events and states of affairs can be illustrated by what Hempel would call an "explanatory sketch" of a specific historical problem.[23] Suppose we take, for this purpose, the state of affairs called British command of the sea in the Napoleonic War, defining the expression "command of the sea" as the state of affairs that exists when a state's military forces maintain that state's own seaborne movements substantially intact while preventing or seriously disrupting seaborne movements by or on behalf of enemy states in war.

In the Napoleonic War, the sea and land forces of Britain wielded command of the sea by performing with a high degree of success the following functions:

(1) the British navy searched out and attacked enemy fleets and sea raiders, and destroyed or drove most of them from the high sea;

(2) British forces captured or drove from the high sea a large proportion of enemy and neutral vessels carrying men and supplies destined for enemy countries;

(3) at certain stages of the war, British naval forces closely blockaded selected enemy ports;

(4) concurrently, British naval forces maintained substantially the seaborne movement of essential supplies to Britain, and covered the transit of British armies to various theaters of military operation overseas; and

(5) British forces deterred enemy forces from attempt-

---

[23] C. G. Hempel, "The Function of General Laws in History," in *Readings in Philosophical Analysis*, pp. 459, 465.

ing seaborne attacks on the British Isles, and deterred or repulsed seaborne operations against British territories overseas.

The British government performed these functions by means of a set of physical instrumentalities and institutions, employed in accordance with certain operational principles. These structures, or patterns, included among others:

(1) naval ships of certain designs operated in certain formations, in accordance with more or less standardized rules;

(2) persons to operate the ships, organized in accordance with certain principles of recruitment, training, authority, and discipline, and exhibiting certain qualities of leadership, morale, etc.;

(3) installations on shore in Britain and at strategic places overseas, to which British ships could go for provisions, rearmament, repairs, and refuge;

(4) garrisons and fortifications to the extent necessary to protect the navy's supporting shore establishments;

(5) physical instrumentalities for production and distribution of capital goods, military equipment, other commodities and services: that is, a national economy; and

(6) a government that maintained order, levied taxes, procured personnel for various purposes, and performed other functions necessary to the maintenance of British seapower as a going concern.

In performing the functions listed, by means of the structures just cited, the British government and its constituency operated within a milieu which included, among other things, the following geographical, political, and other features and properties:

(1) a certain physical layout and configuration of lands and seas, which included the insular British homeland, peninsular Europe, and narrow waterways through which

passed, and had to pass, much of the seaborne traffic between European countries and between Continental Europe and lands overseas;

(2) a certain geographical pattern of the British Empire, which included oversea territories close by some of the most important narrow seas—so-called traffic "bottlenecks"—through which passed, and had to pass, a large part of the seaborne traffic of Britain's Continental enemies;

(3) a certain geographical distribution of political potential (that is, power and influence) upon the earth's surface, characterized in particular by the absence of any strong center of military power outside Europe; and

(4) a certain stage in the development of technology, characterized, among other things, by generally slow and inefficient means of transport overland, by relatively more efficient means of movement by water, and by the absence of any means of movement below or above the surface of the sea.

That the concurrence of the foregoing environmental conditions rendered it possible for the British government to perform the functions defined as command of the sea, by means of the structures cited, is a conclusion which we derive from the following explanatory hypotheses regarding the exercise of naval power in the sailing-ship, pre-railroad, pre-submarine, pre-airpower age:

(1) control of the surface of the sea gave total command of the sea;

(2) the same instrumentalities and operations combined upon the sea the functions of defense and offense, thereby achieving results in proportion to cost rarely, if ever, achievable or even approached by military forces on land;

(3) an insular state enjoyed certain military advantages in a contest for command of the sea, of which the most important was immunity from exposure to invasion across

more or less easily breached land frontiers, and the consequent ability to concentrate its efforts mainly in one form of military force without jeopardizing the safety of the insular homeland;

(4) geographic configuration (such as straits, peninsulas, promontories, wind-patterns, ice-fields, and others) severely limited the routes which sailing ships could navigate successfully, thereby enabling the dominant naval power to command the oceans of the globe as a whole by controlling certain strategic passageways;

(5) states whose geographic location permitted access to the open ocean solely, or mainly, through constricted narrow seas suffered a strategic handicap in comparison with states not so confined;

(6) this handicap was greater before than it was after the development of rapid large-capacity transport overland;

(7) as a result of the mobility and efficiency differential between seaborne and overland transport, a state whose territory was located on the margin of a continental land mass, and whose ships could operate only over sea routes geographically exterior or peripheral to the continent, might nevertheless enjoy in regard to most points on the continental seaboard the advantage of operational centrality;

(8) possession of operating bases near to the bottlenecks of seaborne movement enabled a state's naval forces to remain longer "on station," and thereby multiplied their functional capabilities; and

(9) operating bases which could be approached by hostile forces only from the sea (in consequence of being located on an island, or at the tip of a narrow peninsula, or on a coast backed by desert or jungle), further increased the relative efficiency of dominant naval power, since the same naval forces which denied use of the sea

to the enemy served concomitantly to provide the main defenses of the operating bases overseas.

The foregoing "explanation sketch" does not purport to be a definitive explanation of how it was possible for Britain to command the seas in the Napoleonic period. But it does purport to indicate the form which such an explanation might take as the result of further research and analysis. The sketch comprises the following elements:

(1) a set of statements asserting the occurence of reasonably well-confirmed events comprising a state of affairs called British command of the sea in the Napoleonic period, including statements describing the structures, or means, by which the British government performed the functions that constituted command of the sea;

(2) a set of general explanatory hypotheses (tentative and presumably susceptible of improvement by contraction, or extension, or other revision) which purport to state the salient conditions of command of the sea in the sailing-ship era; and

(3) a set of statements identifying certain features of the milieu in which British command of the sea was established and exercised, features provisionally selected, by inference from the general hypotheses, as necessary and strategic to the state of affairs under consideration.

Such a sketch, and the fuller explanation which one might develop from it, can embody defects of various kinds. The description of the historical state of affairs to be explained may be significantly in error. The general explanatory hypotheses adopted may represent generalizations from too narrow a base of experience, or be untenable or insignificant for other reasons. Or there may be logical errors in the steps by which one determines which aspects of the milieu were necessary and strategic to the occurrence of the state of affairs under consideration. For these and other reasons, we know of no way to avoid some degree of inconclusiveness in explanations of how it was possible for a given historical event or compex state of affairs to have occurred.

However, one can subject his conclusions to various kinds of more or less satisfactory tests. He can try out various alternative hypotheses to ascertain if a more credible and convincing explanation can thereby be derived. Or he can apply the same hypotheses to various subsequent states of the E under consideration. Or he can apply these hypotheses to a different historical E, involving similar, though obviously never identical, phenomena. Or one can try to imagine a hypothetical E, involving the same kinds of issues, which would disconfirm the explanatory hypotheses provisionally selected. When all is said and done, however, one has to accept a certain residual inconclusiveness in most, if not all, explanations of complex states of human affairs.

In the explanation sketch, designed to show how it was possible for a set of functions to be performed by means of a specified set of structures within a specified milieu, we are operating within a frame of analysis very similar to the one designated as possibilism (in Chapter 5). That mode of analysis, it will be recalled, is designed to develop the analyst's own conclusions regarding opportunities and limitations present in the environed unit and in the milieu within which that unit operates. A cardinal postulate of the possibilist doctrine is that properties of unit and milieu may affect the outcome of whatever is undertaken, irrespective of whether or how these limits were consciously perceived and taken into account by the persons who imitated and executed the undertaking under consideration. And that, we emphasize once again, is all that a possibilist mode of analysis—directed to the question: how was it possible for E to occur?—contributes to any historical explanation.

However, most states of affairs, especially those interesting to students of politics, are derived from purposive undertakings. The outcome may or may not have been the one desired and envisaged in advance, but there would have been no undertaking, no course of action, and no operational outcome at all, without purposeful decisions. Thus, as previously emphasized, a satisfactory explanation of most historical puzzles involving human behavior must include explanation of the decisions that determined what would be attempted and by what means.

Those decisions too were necessary conditions of the historical E under consideration. They were as significantly necessary as the environmental matrix within which the subsequent course of events occurred. For the purpose of answering the "how was it possible?" question, considered above, it should be remembered that the decisions are taken as *givens*. In order to "account for" the antecedent decisions, one narrows the focus from all of the significantly necessary conditions of E, to those represented by the decisions only. One asks: how did it come about that the specified decisions were taken from which the subsequent E was derived? This question (often called the "why" question) goes to the values, motivations, purposes, intentions, perceptions, cognition, knowledge, accustomed modes of thinking and deliberating, delineation of alternatives, choice of a course of action, etc., of those persons who entered into the planning and direction of the events that composed the state of affairs under consideration.

Specific decisions of historical personages may be explained with a minimum of formal methodology. Or the effort may involve more complicated apparatus. In either case, one will recognize the analytic perspective previously discussed under the rubric of cognitive behavioralism (in Chapter 7).

Both philosophers of history and behavioral scientists have given attention to what is involved in explaining human actions (choices, decisions, undertakings). We cannot probe very far into this jungle of philosophical and methodological disputation. But we may note salient differences in some of the answers offered to the question: How does one explain, or account for, the purposeful behavior of another person?

One approach to this question is through the process called "empathetic understanding." The essence of this approach can be summed up in two theses: (1) that human history is not merely, or even primarily, an interpretation of observable events, but of the human thought underlying those events; an (2) that the historian gains understanding by himself rethinking—even, in imagination, reliving—the thoughts of the historical personages under consideration.[24]

Hempel, whose own theory of historical explanation is summarized earlier in this chapter, calls empathetic understanding simply a "heuristic device" that functions "to suggest certain psychological hypotheses which might serve as explanatory principles in the case under consideration." By trying "to realize how he himself would act under the given conditions, and under the particular motivations of his heroes," the historian, in effect, "generalizes his findings into a general rule and uses the latter as an explanatory principle in accounting for the actions of the persons involved." Hempel admits that this "de-

[24] In the words of a leading exponent of empathetic understanding, the philosopher R. C. Collingwood, "The history of thought, and therefore all history, is the re-enactment of past thought in the historian's own mind." *The Idea of History*, Oxford University Press, 1946, p. 215. To the same effect, see Benedetto Croce, "History and Chronicle," in *Theories of History*, p. 233.

vice" may be useful, but denies that it is indispensable. "What counts [he insists] is the soundness of the general hypotheses involved, no matter whether they were suggested by empathy or by strictly behavioristic procedure." [25]

Even as a "heuristic device," empathetic understanding poses difficulties. The analyst who purports to view the world through the eyes of another human being can no more escape the handicap imposed by his own subjectivity than can the person whose private universe the analyst is attempting to reconstruct and understand. The analyst, like his subject, is to some degree a prisoner of his own percepts and past experience. The analyst's knowledge of the subject's image of the universe is filtered through his (the analyst's) own sensory organs and through his own screen of motives, prejudices, and other attitudes.

A naïve student of human affairs may attribute to a given person or group, even to one functioning in a milieu radically different from his own, the same values and reactions as he (the analyst) assumes that he himself would experience if he stood in his subject's shoes, so to speak. One even hears it dogmatically asserted that human nature everywhere is the same, and that differences in the past experience of the analyst and of the personage being analyzed do not interpose significant barriers to "empathetic understanding." Yet, as repeatedly emphasized in Chapters 6, 7, and elsewhere, there is impressive evidence that such barriers do exist, that persons of different nationality, even persons playing different roles in the same society, may perceive and react quite differently to surrounding conditions and events. Probing the minds of other persons thus turns out to consist of drawing inferences in accord with some more or less specific,

[25] Hempel, "The Function of General Laws in History," in *Theories of History*, pp. 344, 352.

though inescapably somewhat arbitrary, scale of priorities assigned to different categories of observable behavior—to what the person said and did with reference to the situation confronting him.[26]

But frequently the analyst has access to insufficient verbal or other evidence from which to infer how particular individuals or groups perceived and reacted to their milieu. Or the analyst may distrust the evidence at hand. Such is likely to occur especially in contexts in which (as in competitive games, diplomacy, war, and many other situations) deceit and misrepresentation constitute the normal state of affairs. In such contingencies, it is common practice to resort to generalities—such as, for example, that Napoleon was power-mad, or that Soviet politicians are fanatically committed to spreading communism irrespective of what they may say on particular occasions. When one falls back on such generalities, whether empirically derived or purely conjectural, to explain the actions of a specified person or group, then he has shifted from empirical research to the probabilistic mode of reasoning described in Chapter 6.

This kind of reasoning, which Patrick Gardiner and other philosophers of history call the "dispositional model," sets a person's actions within the "pattern of his normal behavior." Gardiner finds such reasoning especially characteristic of inquiries regarding "desires, intentions, purposes, plans, and programs." With respect to all of

[26] In this connection, we commend readers to reflect on the rules of evidence that have evolved in courts of law for the specific purpose of deducing purpose and intent. The British philosopher W. B. Gallie notes that "a historian, like a jury, may conclude that given certain circumstances the existence of a certain motive or the declaration of a certain purpose or even the receipt of certain information suffices to explain some action, which is therefore conceived as having been at least theoretically predictable." "Explanations in History and the Genetic Sciences," in *Mind*, 1955, v. 64, pp. 160, 175.

these, he says, explanation commonly consists of "fitting a particular action within a certain pattern" which we regard as typical, or normally expectable in the circumstances. We derive notions of what is normally expectable, Gardiner contends, "both from experience of our own behavior *and from experience of the ways other people behave;* and it is in virtue of this that we are able to make the inferences and provide the explanations in question" (italics added).[27]

The italicized phrase identifies one cardinal difference between reasoning from dispositional models and intuiting by empathetic understanding. Exponents of the former contend that anyone's own experience is too narrow a base from which to deduce the motives, intentions, images, and decisional processes of others, a handicap that becomes especially crippling when interpreting the behavior of persons markedly dissimilar from the analyst in cultural heritage, social role, or other differentiating experience.

Any attempt to reconstruct a specified person's image of his milieu and his reactions thereto necessarily involve some use of general behavioral assumptions, analogous to the universal hypotheses, or "covering laws," in Hempel's theory of historical explanation. Without some construct of how the milieu is assumed to appear generally to Soviet politicians, for example, some general ideas as to what they are trying to accomplish, and the character of their intellectual experience and processes, it would scarcely be possible to make any sense of what they say and do. The essential differences between the intuitive empiricism of "empathetic understanding," on the one hand, and reasoning from a "dispositional model," on the other, appear to be mainly differences in research

[27] Patrick Gardiner, *The Nature of Historical Explanation,* Oxford University Press, 1952, p. 125.

perspective [28] and in the level of abstraction at which the explanation is pitched.

At any level of abstraction, the analyst interprets actions (choices, decisions) in the light of some kind of explanatory behavioral hypotheses. These may be stated explicitly or left more or less implicit. If the latter, it may be because the analyst has not formulated them explicitly himself, or because he regards them as "truisms" which everybody is presumed to know and take for granted.[29]

Since this aspect of explanation involves drawing up an account of how it came about that a given decision or set of decisions was taken, and since decisions are always taken in some context, there is no escape from dealing somehow with the decision-maker's demonstrated, inferred, or presumed image of his milieu and his mode of reacting thereto. In the main, we repeat, explanations of reasons for decisions usually exhibit some mixture of the analytical patterns previously examined in Chapters 6 and 7. Whether the one or the other, or some blend of the two, will depend in a particular instance on the level of specificity of conclusions required, on the amount and kind of historical evidence available, and also on the conceptual tools and techniques that the analyst employs and to which he is accustomed.

[28] William Dray, for example, objects that reasoning from a dispositional model is sheer "spectatorism" that ignores the viewpoint of the person whose behavior is being explained. *Laws and Explantion in History,* Oxford University Press, 1957, pp. 142*ff.*

[29] On this point, see Michael Scriven, "Truisms as the Grounds for Historical Explanations," in *Theories of History,* pp. 443*ff.*

9

MAN-MILIEU RELATIONSHIPS RECONSID-
ERED IN THE CONTEXT OF PREDICTION

WE TURN now to man-milieu relationships in the context
of prediction. The first point to be noted here is the negative posture of many historians, and even some geographers and political scientists. Their argument runs somewhat as follows: Human behavior is unique; no two milieux are alike; history never repeats; hence it is futile
to try to predict events, and particularly futile to predict the specific reactions of particular people; one cannot "pinpoint" the future; therefore, the argument concludes, the student of human affairs should concentrate
on historical descriptions that enrich "understanding."

No one could believe more strongly than we that the
historical study of any subject is intellectually rewarding.
But to take refuge in history because one cannot "pinpoint" the future is to misconceive the nature of predic-
ton and the uses everyone inescapably makes of it in
the business of living. The issue is not whether to predict or not to predict. The issue is rather what one may
profitably try to predict, and how to go about it.

One misconception derives from a supposed requirement of certainty. It is sometimes contended that an explanatory hypothesis, empirical generalization, or inductive law, is useless unless it is invariably verified by
events. According to this posture, one exception, one instance in which verification fails, invalidates the law and
renders it useless as a predictive tool. Since 100 per cent
verification is rare in human undertakings and achievements, this all-or-nothing attitude reduces the social uni-

verse to a congeries of unique objects and events, a universe of "isolated facts" that "allow no prediction at all."[1]

This all-or-nothing posture is patently contrary to everyday experience, as well as to the basic tenets of modern science. Speaking in the context of psychological theory (but in words applicable to the whole spectrum of human affairs), Egon Brunswik has said: "The acceptance of ambiguity of prediction as a legitimate and general feature of psychological results will probably meet with the same resistance which logicians had to face when they proceeded from a dichotomous true-false alternative to multivalued logic, or which empirical scientists had to face when developing out of theological and metaphysical stages into the positive stage."[2]

One can arrange all imaginable predictive statements regarding a specified contingency along a continuum, of which one pole would be "certainty" and the other, "impossibility." Most of the statements would fall within the zone expressible by the advert *probably*. We shall return to this idea later in the chapter. For the moment we merely record our agreement in general with the position of Jacob Bronowski: human affairs develop in patterns that are more or less uncertain, but in a more or less calculable way.[3]

Neither the statesman, nor the government intelligence analyst, nor the academic student of politics can escape the future. Every opinion, every proposal for action, every decision regarding NATO, Middle Eastern oil, communism in Latin America, or any other issue of foreign re-

---

[1] Egon Brunswik, "The Probability Point of View," in *Psychological Theory*, edited by M. H. Marx, Macmillan, 1951, p. 200.

[2] *Ibid.*, pp. 200-1.

[3] Jacob Bronowski, *The Common Sense of Science*, Harvard University Press, 1953, p. 87.

lations reflects some image of the future, some set of expectations as to how proposed solutions might affect the shape of things to come.

In this respect, the practice of statecraft and the study of statecraft are no different from other sectors of human affairs. Human actions are characteristically oriented towards the future, only rarely towards the past. We do not expect the future to be exactly like the past. But we do "assume that the future will have some general likeness with futures we have met before. . . ." These expectations reflect our stock of working hypotheses— hunches, common sense, assumptions, principles, now and then explicit propositions—about the nature and properties of ourselves and our milieu. Such guides to everyday living are analogous to the more formal "laws" of science.[4]

Expectations, whether explicitly formulated or left implicit, will be recognized as similar to the explanatory hypotheses, generalizations, and laws that underlie most formal explanations of historical events. Indeed, it has repeatedly been asserted that the "logical structures" of explanation and prediction are very similar, if not identical.[5] As previously noted, explanation, conceived as a logical process, involves determining the necessary and/or sufficient conditions of a specified past event or state of affairs, by means of deductive inference from empirical generalizations (inductive premises) or deductive theories. Prediction involves the same logical steps. Either one cal-

[4] *Ibid.*, pp. 104, 113, 114.
[5] For example, Herbert Feigl, "Notes on Causality," in *Readings in the Philosophy of Science*, edited by H. Feigl and M. Brodbeck, Appleton-Century-Crofts, 1953, p. 417; Patrick Gardiner, *The Nature of Historical Explanation*, Oxford University Press, 1952, pp. 2-3; C. G. Hempel, "The Function of General Laws in History," in *Readings in Philosophical Analysis*, edited by H. Feigl and W. Sellars, Appleton-Century-Crofts, 1949, p. 462.

culates, by inference from inductive premises or deductive theories, the necessary conditions of the occurrence of a hypothetical future event or state of affairs; or else one calculates the event or state of affairs that will probably, or must certainly, result from a *given* (actual or hypothetical) set of conditions. There are, however, important practical differences between historical explanation and prediction.

In the former, the event or state of affairs to be explained—the given E—has already occurred, and belongs to the unchangeable past. The milieu within which E occurred also belongs to that same unchangeable past. The task in explaining E is to deduce from some general hypothesis, or set of hypotheses, which features of that milieu were necessary and/or sufficient to the occurrence of E.

Competent scholars may differ in their interpretations of historical evidence. They may reason from different, even contradictory, general hypotheses regarding the nature of man and of man-milieu relationships in general. They may employ contradictory topical hypotheses respecting which features of the milieu were necessary and strategic to the specified E under consideration.

If, for these or other reasons, differences of interpretation emerge, there is no court of final jurisdiction in a free society to decide which description of the historical milieu is the "correct" one, or to rule that one set of explanatory hypotheses accounts more acceptably, or credibly, or convincingly for E than another. Hence there is a certain inconclusiveness about all historical explanations. Interpretations that satisfy one historian may seem unconvincing to others of the same or a later generation.

Another kind of inconclusiveness pervades prediction. Predictions are statements of future relationships between specified variables in accordance with specified explanatory hypotheses. Events may confirm the prediction as stated. Or the prediction may be disconfirmed because the necessary conditions failed to develop as assumed. Or the predicted event may occur, but because of some set of conditions other than those postulated as necessary and strategic. In any case, the occurrence of the predicted E is contingent on a state of the milieu which too has not come into existence, and which can be calculated only within some range of indeterminacy.

Those differences are reflected in the kinds of questions one asks about the past and about the future. With respect to the past, our thesis has been that a satisfactory explanation usually involves answering the question: How was it possible for E to occur? And if decisions were among the necessary and strategic conditions of E, then explanation also involves answering the second question: How did it come about that those particular decisions were taken? Only rarely, as we noted earlier, do serious scholars try to demonstrate that what did happen had to happen; and, we repeat, such attempts have been invariably inconclusive because deterministic hypotheses cannot be satisfactorily confirmed or refuted with respect to a history that cannot be repeated.

The kinds of questions one asks about the future, and the kinds of predictive statements one makes, may depend on whether the problem in hand is policy-oriented or not. In order to make a contemplative, non-policy-oriented prediction, one takes a set of existing conditions, projects them into the future with or without modification, and deduces their effects from general inductive premises (hypotheses, theories, laws). In making a policy-oriented prediction, one starts with a given E to be achieved, and deduces from inductive premises what changes in the milieu and/or in the environed unit must occur in order for E to be achieved.

This practical difference should not obscure the logical similarity of contemplative and policy-oriented predictions. Every policy-oriented prediction can be transmuted into a contemplative prediction. Thus: "In order to achieve E, do C," becomes: "If C is done, E will be achieved." We shall give some examples of these types in a moment.

The distinction between contemplative and policy-oriented analysis is meaningless in the context of historical explanation. How one interprets the past may affect his attitude toward the future. But past events are finished. One can try to "account for" them; but one cannot change them. Unless one is a strict determinist, he will normally make the opposite assumption about the future. Only strict determinism postulates man's inability, on empirical grounds, to choose among alternatives and thereby to shape in some degree the course of future events.

The distinction between policy-oriented and contemplative predictions may be useful in any sector of human affairs. This distinction is especially important in the more policy-oriented fields, of which political science is in general probably the most policy-oriented of all.

Non-policy-oriented predictions generally take one of two forms. Either the statement predicts that a *specific event or state of affairs* will occur, or will probably occur, or may possibly occur; or it predicts (with similar gradations from certainty to uncertainty) a *future state of the milieu* which sets the limits of possible variation of a specified class of phenomena. Since an E specifically predicted can occur only within the limits set by the milieu and by the characters of the environed unit, predictions of the second type may be identical with some of the environmental assumptions on which predictions of the first type are explicitly or implicitly contingent.

PREDICTION

Demographic projections provide illustrative examples of both types and their interrelations. For this purpose let us consider the study entitled *The Future Population of Europe and the Soviet Union,* by F. W. Notestein and other members of the Office of Population Research of Princeton University.[6] This work begins with a precise description of the logical structure and procedures involved in making the projections presented. These projections purport to demonstrate what the population of Europe and the Soviet Union (as a whole, subregions of the whole, and specific countries) would be by 1970, *if* certain assumed conditions should prevail.

The "major assumptions" are two: (1) "that the trends of the vital [birth and death] rates up to 1970 will represent orderly developments of those in the interwar [1919-1939] period"; and (2) "that no migration takes place over the 1937 national borders of Europe between the base censuses and 1970." These two assumptions set the limits of variation within which the 1970 population estimates are calculated.

These major assumptions were derived quite differently. The "no migration" assumption is arbitrary, and is presumed to be contrary to what will actually happen. It was introduced "because of the impossibility of making any realistic estimate concerning future migrations, which will depend on, among other things, postwar boundaries and political arrangements [which in 1944 were still highly uncertain]. However, the assumption has the virtue of permitting the projections to reflect the natural sources of future growth."

The "orderly development" assumption was derived apparently by logical inference from past experience. The "demographic effects of the war" were ignored "because

[6] Published in 1944 by Princeton University Press, for the League of Nations.

· 181 ·

of the impossibility of giving quantitative expression to the losses of a conflict still in progress [in 1944]." But that decision was "justified" on the hypothesis that "changes brought about by the war are not likely to alter the fundamental demographic position of the major regions studied." This hypothesis was derived from the experience of the past, that "the underlying trends of vital rates have shown considerable stability," via the further hypothesis that "the most practicable assumption is that the new world will grow out of the old in a somewhat orderly fashion."

These "major assumptions," together with several lesser ones (for example, regarding the validity of census data), provide the matrix within which, by recognized logical steps, the projections are derived. These are described as "valid working models of the results to be expected from a continuation of recent vital trends. As such they are broadly predictive." But (and here the authors of the study are very emphatic) the projections "can be converted into realistic predictions only when it becomes possible to superimpose the effects of the war and of postwar migrations, and when the nature of [postwar] population policies become apparent." Then comes the punch line: "As predictions of actual future events, such projections will be no more valid than their underlying assumptions, however useful they may be as analytical devices illustrating the dynamics of population change." [7]

Non-policy-oriented predictions may rest in part on certain assumptions about future policy. For example, a prediction that nuclear power will probably displace other energy converters in electric power plants by 1980 would involve making assumptions not only with reference to engineering developments but also with reference to business and/or government decisions. *But the embodi-*

[7] *Ibid.*, pp. 20, 21, 43.

ment of policy assumptions does not per se *make a prediction policy-oriented.* That is to say, the prediction may rest in part upon a policy assumption, but it does not thereby become policy-oriented unless it is part of a policy-forming process.

Contemplative prediction—that a specified event may occur—may set in motion a policy-forming process, even though the prediction itself is not policy-oriented. Such a policy-forming process may be activated expressly to invalidate or to confirm the prediction, and may in fact do so. Students of politics are familiar with supposed "bandwagon" and "underdog" effects of public opinion polls and election forecasts. But similar effects have been observed in many other areas: for example, in demographic projections, business forecasts, and crop estimates. Thus, published predictions of a business recession might be followed by governmental or other actions designed expressly to prevent the predicted state of affairs from coming to pass.[8]

[8] The social effects of public predictions have evoked a good deal of controversy. The philosopher-logician Herbert Feigl says: "The one remarkable feature in which social-science predictions differ from those in the natural sciences is the well-known fact that once these predictions have been divulged, their very existence (that is, their being taken cognizance of) may upset the original prediction. It seems at present problematic as to whether it is possible to devise something like a method of convergent successive approximations, in order to take account of the effect of divulged predictions, and thus to obviate the notorious difficulty." *Readings in the Philosophy of Science,* p. 418. Others, equally qualified to speak on this issue, are less pessimistic. See, for example, Emile Grunberg and Franco Modigliani, "The Predictability of Social Events," in *Journal of Political Economy,* 1954, v. 62, pp. 465*ff;* and H. A. Simon, "Bandwagon and Underdog Effects and the Possibility of Election Predictions," in *Public Opinion Quarterly,* 1954, v. 18, pp. 245*ff.* We are especially indebted to Professor Harold Guetzkow (of Northwestern University) for suggesting further attention than we gave to this issue in our earlier essay, *Man-Milieu Relationship Hypotheses in the Context of International Politics.*

PREDICTION

Predictions that are genuinely policy-oriented exhibit certain other practical differences. A responsible decision-maker has a manipulative interest in the future. He desires not merely to find out how things are likely to work; he also wants to make them work to suit his own particular purposes. Predictive operations connected with policy-making tend to consist mainly of calculating what functions must be performed if the envisaged policy objective is to be realized; whether and how such functions can be performed; etc.

Like historical explanation, policy-oriented prediction involves deducing the necessary and strategic conditions of a *known E*—in the historical case, an *E* that has already occurred; in the policy case, an *E* that is defined more or less precisely but has not yet occurred. Unlike historical explanation and unlike contemplative prediction, too, policy-oriented prediction involves calculating both the technical *possibility* and the *cost* of *changing the milieu* through time to the extent required to bring into existence and to maintain the conditions deduced to be necessary and strategic for the occurrence of the envisaged but still-to-be-realized state of affairs.

Some idea of what is involved in this type of prediction can be illustrated by a simple prediction-sketch, similar to the explanation-sketch which we attempted in connection with historical explanation. Let us suppose a given policy objective is to encourage more foreign tourists to visit the United States. Let us suppose further that investigation indicates that the principal deterrents include (1) resentment against the administrative red-tape involved in getting into the United States, and (2) considerable difficulty in acquiring sufficient dollar currency.

Given this description of the present state of affairs, the predictive problem can be stated as: what can be done to change the milieu so as to encourage tourism? The answer will depend, first of all, on the analyst's "theory of the problem." Let us imagine that it runs about as follows: In every country a certain number of people yearn to travel and visit new and strange places, and some of them have the necessary means (in their own currency) to do so; in making their plans, most of them will choose those countries which offer exciting experiences, and make it relatively easy for foreign visitors to come and go. Applying these premises to the problem in hand, one might infer that more tourists will be encouraged to visit the United States, *if* border formalities are reduced and simplified, and *if* the United States offers various tourists subsidies in the form of reduced rates, etc.

In this prediction-sketch, the issue is not what actions *will* (certainly, or probably, or possibly) be taken, as would be the issue in a simple contemplative prediction. Nor is the issue what actions *should* be taken, a question that would transfer the problem from the realm of prediction to that of decision. The issue is rather what actions, *if taken,* are likely to realize the future state of affairs defined in advance as the objective of policy. The problem, in short, is to determine what changes in the milieu are necessary and strategic to the realization of the given policy objective, a problem that is solved by means of inference from suitable inductive premises.

Conceivably, further research and analysis may appear to justify a further prediction that the envisaged end is certainly, or probably, unattainable with any means available. Such a conclusion may lead to revision of the policy objective to bring it into better balance with the means at one's command. In the above policy problem, for example, one might conclude that it would probably be impossible to persuade Congress to relax border formalities or to enact tourist subsidies.

As shown in the example drawn from demography

and in the sketch just above, all predictions involve making assumptions about the future. No matter how the prediction is phrased, it can always be rephrased (unless it is a purely random choice) somewhat as follows: If such-and-such changes take place in the milieu and/or if such-and-such decisions are taken, then such-and-such event or state of affairs will certainly, or will probably, or may possibly occur.

Assumptions on which predictions are based may be derived in at least two ways. The analyst may make purely arbitrary assumptions, even ones presumed to be contrary to future facts. Doing so enables him to concentrate on other aspects of the process under consideration. Suppose, for example, one desires to analyze the relationship, if any, between population change and the relative military capabilities of states. In order to evaluate the demographic variable, one may desire to focus specifically on that one factor. In order to do this, one might proceed from some such hypothesis as: If other environmental factors do not change, the military capabilities of states will vary in proportion to changes in their respective populations. The *ceteris paribus* assumption is arbitrary. The odds are overwhelmingly against its validation by future events. But it is an analytic device, employed in every science. This device is employed in the "no migration" assumption of the demographic model discussed above. Arbitrary assumptions are employed in policy and strategy analysis, especially in the context of training. For example, it is understood to be common practice to work out military problems on alternate sets of purely hypothetical and often quite arbitrary assumptions as to enemies and allies, theaters of operation, weapons, and tactics, etc.

Frequently, however, especially in connection with specific policy problems, there is need to anticipate as accurately as possible what the future state of certain environmental factors will be like. Suppose the problem is to formulate a policy regarding industrial applications of nuclear energy during the next ten years. In this context, it might be desired to anticipate the probable trends in costs and availabilities of other forms of energy during this time-span. For such a purpose a purely arbitrary assumption plainly will not suffice. One needs rather to estimate as closely as possible what the future state of affairs will be like in this respect. Such an estimate is a prediction, derived by the same logical steps as any other prediction. Such an estimate may be called an assumption, too. But it is an assumption in two different senses. First, it is an assumption in the sense that the estimate, once made, is not subjected to further testing but is treated as if it were satisfactorily confirmed for purposes of the problem in hand. Second, it is assumed for purposes of the problem that the estimate will in fact be confirmed by events.

By means of arbitrary and/or inductively derived assumptions, one constructs a hypothetical future state of the milieu of a given environed unit (individual, organized group, or some other). Among other things, this hypothetical milieu may include assumptions: (1) that certain specified phenomena will remain constant during the time-span under consideration; (2) that certain other non-human phenomena will change in specified ways as a result of "natural" and/or "social" processes; and (3) that the human components of the environed unit's milieu will behave in certain predicted ways.

With such a construct, or hypothetical model of the future milieu, one can perform predictively the whole range of operations previously discussed under the rubrics of probabilism and possibilism. By means of a probabilistic behavioral model, he can predict the environed unit's decisions and undertakings. By means of possibilistic hypotheses, he can estimate the probable operational results of *given* undertakings. He can also estimate opportunities and limitations implicit, or latent, in the milieu, with respect to various alternative undertakings. And he can calculate what further changes in the milieu would have to occur in order for certain given undertakings to achieve the end in view.

Major decisions of foreign policy always turn on some such construct of the future. Consider, for example, the United States opposition to Anglo-French military intervention in the early stage of the Suez crisis of 1956. From materials available to the public, one might reconstruct somewhat as follows the assumptions *apparently* underlying the American decision to oppose the use of force against Egypt. Such intervention would involve risk of Soviet counterintervention, and hence of bringing on a general war ruinous to everybody; even if the Soviet Union should remain nominally neutral, Anglo-French military action against Egypt would arouse hostile feelings all over the Arab world, in India, Indonesia, and elsewhere, with more or less disastrous repercussions for the West; even if negotiations should fail to achieve a satisfactory solution promptly, the United States and the West European states would not be left without alternatives; the economy of Egypt was notoriously weak and dependent on foreign markets and goods; disruption of economic relations with Europe and America would worsen Egypt's desperate internal conditions, and put heavy pressure on the Egyptian government; the Soviet Union probably would not, and perhaps could not, provide aid on a scale sufficient to sustain the Egyptian economy through a long-drawn-out economic struggle; moreover, only as a going concern would the Canal be an economic asset to Egypt; in the long run, the Egyptian government could have no rational interest in closing the Canal or denying its use to the shipping of the principal users; even if President Nasser should irrationally close the Canal, or be unable to maintain service through it, alternative shipping routes, though longer and more costly, did nevertheless exist; if such a state of affairs should develop, the United States could provide financial and other support necessary to sustain the West European economies until a satisfactory solution could be worked out. The above sketch may or may not be an accurate summary of the American official position and its underlying assumptions. Accuracy is not the point at issue here. The point is rather that the American decision (unless a purely random choice, which of course it was not) rested upon *some such set of assumptions* regarding the future; and that these assumptions, in turn, consisted of predictions which (unless they were random guesses) involved the logical steps previously described. In this respect, too, policy-oriented and non-policy-oriented predictions are similar. All predictions, as stated some paragraphs back, can be rephrased as: If such-and-such changes take place in the milieu, and/or if such-and-such decisions are taken, then such-and-such event or state of affairs will certainly, or will probably, or may possibly occur.

If the predicted event is a decision, the predictive statement may be phrased in terms of degrees of probability, but never plausibly in terms of absolute certainty or inevitability. This is so because the concept of decision implies by definition an act of choice among alternatives; and choice is inconsistent with the environmental or other determinism from which alone one could deduce a future decision as certain or inevitable.

This brings us to one of the most important points in this whole discussion. Loose forms of speaking often appear to contradict the rule stated just above. When President Eisenhower ordered U.S. Marines ashore in Lebanon in 1958, it was frequently asserted in the press and elsewhere that the disturbed state of Lebanese politics and the possibly explosive repercussions throughout the Near East *left him no alternative*. Such assertions were made repeatedly in defense of President Kennedy's order to Khrushchev to remove Soviet missiles from Cuba. At the critical juncture of American neutrality in the First World War, President Wilson told the German government that, unless it abandoned its unrestricted submarine campaign against merchant vessels, "the Government of the United States can have no choice but to sever diplomatic relations. . . ."

Scarcely a month passes but one reads or hears of some statesman having no choice but to do so-and-so. Strictly construed, *all such statements are nonsense*. Unless most politicians, government officials, journalists, academicians, and others who express opinions about public affairs are genuine convinced determinists (which they patently are not), they do not mean what they say. What such deterministic statements appear usually to mean is simply that the speaker regards alternative choices not as impossible but as unacceptable. And very frequently, one suspects, deterministic forms of speech are utilized deliberately to serve forensic propaganda purposes.

Now, in the light of the foregoing paragraphs, let us arrange predictive statements regarding a hypothetical future decision x along a scale as follows:

(1) x certainly will not be taken;
(2) x almost certainly will not be taken;
(3) x probably will not be taken;
(4) x may or may not be taken;
(5) x probably will be taken;

(6) *x* almost certainly will be taken;
(7) *x* certainly will (or inevitably must) be taken.

Unless one really is a "simon-pure" determinist (and we reiterate that we have never met one), he eliminates statements (1) and (7), at the two poles, as incompatible with the assumption of human capacity to choose among alternatives. If we eliminate these deterministic extremes, the remaining statements represent calculations (more precisely, estimations) along a sort of continuum of the odds for or against occurrence of the decision-*x* under consideration. The odds, as estimated, may run weakly or strongly towards one pole or the other; they may even approach certainty. But some degree of indeterminacy, or uncertainty, always remains. One cannot expurgate indeterminacy from the concept of choice!

This element of indeterminacy also applies, if the prediction relates to a state of affairs contingent on a given decision. This is so, even if the decision was taken without reference to, or knowledge of, the relevant environmental factors. In the case of the man approaching the open manhole in total darkness (page 95 above), an observer could predict that the actor *A* would fall into the manhole—but only on the assumption that *A* did not stop or alter his course before reaching it. The observer would not be justified in totally disregarding those contingencies, even though it was certain that *A* was totally unaware of the open manhole. The observer might estimate the odds of *A* going into the hole as *almost* certain. But some element of indeterminacy would still remain.

Since virtually every ongoing problem interesting to the student of politics involves predicting decisions *and/or* the operational results of decisions, the element of uncertainty implicit in the decision itself extends to the state of affairs contingent on the decision. Thus, for this reason if for no other, one is never justified in making statements regarding the actions and relations of states in any terms stronger than some degree of probability.

However, it may be useful for various reasons to estimate relationships on the assumption that certain decisions will be taken. Such an assumption may be arbitrary, or it may be a product of the most careful attempt to deduce probable future decisions. In either case, by taking certain policy objectives and strategies as *given* for purposes of analysis, one can concentrate on the possibilities (that is, the estimated operational results) of the decisions thus assumed.

This procedure brings to bear the analytical frame and general hypothesis of possibilism: to wit, that environmental limitations exist, and that at least some of these may be operative with respect to any *given* course of action undertaken, *irrespective* of whether or how these limitations are perceived and reacted to by the decision-makers in the case under consideration. For the student of international politics, the above procedure is directly relevant to the task of estimating the military or other capabilities that are likely to become manifest in interactions of power, influence, and deference among states.

In applying this rule, however, one must also keep in mind that no analyst is omniscient. Estimates of the capabilities of states may be expressed in terms of what is possible, or in terms of what is more or less probable, under given policy assumptions; but one is rarely, if ever, justified in making capability estimates that approach even closely to the pole of certainty, or inevitability.

One may recall, in this connection, the predictions during World War II, sometimes phrased in terms of certainty or near-certainty, that Nazi Germany could not stand the financial and moral strains of a long war; that the Red Army would certainly collapse within a few weeks under the hammer-blows of the Wehrmacht; that the French army was the best in Europe; that the British nation could not survive the "blitz"; and many other predictions equally dogmatic. One can also recall more recent dogmatic predictions regarding the capabilities of the Soviet Union, Red China, the United States, or other nations, some of which have already been disconfirmed by events. Such predictive failures pose difficult questions. How does one react to dogmatic capability estimates or other predictions by Professor *A*, or the Central Intelligence Agency, or some other presumably expert person or organization? How does one determine the credibility (that is to say, the presumptive tenability) of predictions as yet neither confirmed nor disconfirmed by events? Must one simply judge such predictions by the reputation of the predictor? [9] Is the only feasible alternative a posture of cynical skepticism? The answer is no to both questions—provided one has the necessary knowledge and analytical skill to perform the predictive operations himself.

Suppose the problem is to test the credibility of a predictive thesis that has been a premise of British statecraft since 1957. In that year, in the Government's annual "statement on defense," it was asserted that the people of Britain could not be defended against the "consequences of an attack with nuclear weapons." For obvious reasons no simple test of this prediction is feasible. Such confirmation or disconfirmation as is possible consists of breaking up the prediction as a whole into more elemental propositions which have been, or could be, subjected to empirical testing. Such propositions would relate, among other

[9] This is close to the position reached by Olaf Helmer and Nicholas Rescher in their paper, "On the Epistemology of the Inexact Sciences," Publication No. P-1513, October 13, 1958, The RAND Corporation.

things, in the given problem, to the properties of nuclear explosives, to the capabilities of planes and other means of delivering nuclear warheads, and to the potentialities of defensive instrumentalities and techniques.

With respect to nuclear explosives and explosions, there is a vast accumulation of experience, some of it classified, but much of it in the public domain and available to anyone competent to interpret it. There are data regarding the blast, heat, and radioactivity generated by explosions of various types and magnitudes, regarding the area and distribution of radioactive fallout, regarding the duration of residual radioactivity of various kinds, regarding the immediate and delayed effects of human exposure to radioactive material, etc.

With respect to delivery systems, there is also a great deal of accumulated information. Such information includes the range and carrying capacities of planes of various types, the properties of ballistic missiles, the use of submarines as launching platforms, the design and operational characteristics of the delivery systems of particular military services, etc.

With respect to local defense against attacks with nuclear weapons, tests under simulated conditions of war have yielded conclusions as to the odds of attacking formations and units eluding or breaking through various kinds and concentrations of defenses (interceptor planes, gun and rocket barrages, defensive missile systems, etc.). There is at least some information regarding the properties of so-called "hardened" missile installations. One could derive from past disaster experience some estimate of a given people's behavior under attack, the efficiency of fallout shelters, fire-fighting systems, evacuation plans, medical care of radiation victims, anti-contamination techniques, emergency communication systems, and other survival schemes. Such experience could be evaluated with special reference to the British milieu (in the problem stated), with special consideration given to the country's area, density of habitation, size and functional relations of the great conurbations, their proximity to the sea, vulnerability of the transportation and communication grids, strength and direction of prevailing winds, and many other features of the milieu.

It is, of course, to accumulate more information on these and other aspects of nuclear attack and defense that tests of many kinds are run in laboratories, on proving grounds, and (under simulated conditions of attack and disaster) in cities and larger areas. But such information has no significance *per se*. It acquires significance to the problem only as the data are ordered and interpreted within some frame of concepts and explanatory propositions (hypotheses, premises). Broadly speaking, in the given problem, the task is mainly—though by no means exclusively—one of describing certain nonhuman phenomena, and of formulating and applying explanatory hypotheses as to the opportunities and limitations latent in those phenomena, viewed within a given social context.

Elsewhere in the same British defense statement, it was further asserted that "the only existing safeguard against major aggression is the power to threaten retaliation with nuclear weapons. . . ." How is this prediction to be evaluated? The analytical problem here is not primarily one of estimating capabilities (that is, the odds of survival under postulated operational contingencies), but of predicting decisions. The phenomena to be evaluated consist not of the properties of explosives or other predominantly nonhuman factors, but rather a set of expectations (that is, predictions) regarding the purposes, perceptions, reactions, and decisions of adverse parties.

From the standpoint of those responsible for British

defense policy, as for sideline observers who try to inter-pret and anticipate events, the existence of the Soviet Union, the location of strategic target areas therein, their distance from British airbases, etc., are relevant facts. The same may be said of Russian attitudes and reactions, as these are apperceived by British statesmen. When the British Minister of Defense asserts that the Soviet govern-ment will behave in a specified manner—that is, be deterred from "major aggression"—by British possession of nuclear weapons, certain means of delivering them, and a threat to retaliate, he is predicting a future state of the milieu by reference to some image of what is normally expectable behavior on the part of Soviet decision-makers in the envisaged contingency.

Manifestly, such a prediction regarding future Soviet behavior is not susceptible to the kind of verification that one might employ to establish the existence of the Soviet Union, or to establish the geographic location of Britain, or to establish the properties of nuclear explosives. The premise that the Russians will be effectively deterred is no more susceptible to full-scale testing *in toto* than is the prediction that Britain could not be defended against "the consequences of an attack with nuclear weapons."

What the observer can do is to compare his own with the image of probable Soviet behavior, expressed in the British document. In doing so he will almost certainly judge the relevance and significance of what Russian statesmen say and do, and he will just as certainly fill in gaps where evidence is lacking, by resort to general no-tions of how Russians typically act and react; and he will almost certainly derive such notions by generalizing past observations of Soviet behavior in the context of Russian history and Communist doctrine. As we have emphasized in Chapter 6 (on probabilistic behavioral models), such a model (whatever else it may include) almost certainly embodies assumptions regarding the decision-maker's purposes (that is, policy objectives), his image of the milieu in which he is operating, and his mode of utilizing such knowledge in framing strategies that he deems to be feasible as well as compatible with his scheme of values.

In the illustrative case, the British Government's policy statement does not delineate explicitly the behavioral assumptions on which the strategy of deterrence is based. Let us imagine, for the purpose of the example, that their reasoning ran as follows: Soviet rulers are committed to expansion, political and ideological as well as territorial; they will not hesitate to employ force to attain their ends if they believe they can do so without too great risk; they will not be deterred by international norms, legal or moral, but only by counterthreats backed up by effective force; they may be presumed to have generally reliable information as to the state of Western (including British) weapons, delivery systems, and degree of readiness for action; and they may be presumed also to apply such knowledge rationally in deciding what risks to take and what course of action to follow.

If some such reasoning did *in fact* underlie the British policy statement, no critic can prove conclusively that this was not a correct description of Soviet behavior. The most that the critic can do is to test his subject's conclusions against his own or some other critic's judgments. How nearly correct either the actor's or the critics' judgment is may eventually be tested by events. Short of that, everything depends on the skill, or expertise, with which past experience is generalized into propositions about future behavior.[10]

One way of resolving the difficulty of predicting specific choices is to deduce probable choices (both as to objec-

[10] On the concept and function of "expert" opinion, see *ibid*.

tives and as to strategy) from estimated capabilities. This technique is said to be standard practice in military education and in the planning of military operations. One suspects that it also enters into diplomatic and other political planning, and likewise into the judgments of journalists and other sideline observers of the international scene.

The essence of this method is to begin by estimating what courses of action a given decision-making unit (military command, foreign office, head of government, or other) is capable of undertaking with fair prospect of success. The next step is to assume that the unit will choose rationally from the range of presumptively achievable alternatives a strategy which offers relatively high promise of success. The third step is to assume that the unit being analyzed will evaluate its own capabilities in the same way as the outsider making the analysis. From these assumptions, the latter calculates the range within which the decision will probably fall—by the process of himself (the analyst) estimating the possibilities latent in the operational milieu.

The fruitfulness of this line of reasoning, it is obvious, must depend in part on the tenability of the assumptions outlined above. Anyone who has read this far will realize how dubious one or more of those assumptions are likely to be. Nevertheless, inference of intentions from estimates of the relative capabilities of the interacting units may provide a fruitful first approximation.

Another way to evade the refractory problem of predicting specific decisions is to resort to negative prediction. By means of the same logical procedures, it may be possible to narrow the range within which a specific decision seems likely to fall. By application of suitable premises, one attempts to eliminate as *very improbable* those choices which would represent the greatest deviation from the postulated norm. He then narrows the range still further by eliminating as *quite improbable* those choices which represent progressively smaller deviations from the postulated norm. At some point he decides that it is too speculative, with evidence at hand, to carry this narrowing process any further. What is left is a *residual range of variation* within which the specific choice seems likely to fall. Thus, if one cannot forecast precisely what the British Cabinet will do about nuclear weapons during the next ten years, he can perhaps reach more general conclusions as to some of the choices that they are more or less likely *not* to make.

The rationale of this procedure is self-evident. The margin of probable error is assumed to increase as one moves from the most improbable to the most probable pole of the range of all conceivable choices. Whether such an assumption is tenable depends, of course, on the knowledge and insight (that is, the expertise) that have gone into setting up the model of normally expectable decision-making. That is to say, negative prediction, to narrow the range of probable choice, no less than for positive prediction to "spot" a specific choice, involves the application of general propositions as to what is typical or normally expectable behavior by the decision-making unit under consideration. But negative prediction does bypass the issue of specific choices (in predicting which the probability of error may be so high as to nullify the value of the whole operation), in favor of a less specific solution involving considerably lower probability of error.

In recognizing the fruitlessness of deterministic predictions (represented by such verbalisms as "will certainly" or "must inevitably"), and by acknowledging the indeterminacy in predictions based on "odds of occurrence," one need not conclude that all predictions about man-milieu relationships are sheer guesswork. Between the extremes of predictive certainty and total unpredictability, as we have repeatedly emphasized, lies the concept of "degree of probability" with respect both to choices and decisions, and to operational outcomes, or level of performance. The whole trend of our argument is that this concept, and the man-milieu relationships frameworks into which it is incorporated, constitute useful and widely used intellectual tools for estimating within some range of indeterminacy the boundaries and patterns of things to come.

10

THE ISSUES REVIEWED

THE FOREGOING examination of ecological perspective and ideas was undertaken with two related purposes in view. One was to identify and clarify the various modes of thinking and speaking about environment and environmental relationships. The second purpose, subsidiary to the first, was to exemplify the utilities and limitations of ecological concepts and theories in various social contexts, but especially in the context of international politics.

We observed that those who conduct international statecraft, as well as those who write and teach about it, seem generally to take for granted that the policies of governments, the power, influence, and prestige of nation-states, and the patterns of international political relations are significantly associated with phenomena variously called the arena, stage, setting, environment, milieu, or situation. We observed that the words and phrases regularly used to denote such relationships are in general the same as those used to denote the relationships of an individual to his environment. We observed also that speakers seem rarely to be much concerned with, or even aware of, the instrumental mechanisms and processes that alone give meaning to assertions of environmental relationships. It was likewise evident that the fanciful, teleological rhetoric to which many interpreters of political events are addicted tends to obscure those instrumental connections, or even to bypass them altogether. We observed further how accepted usage has the effect (whatever the speaker's intent) of reifying abstract entities, such as the state, political system, and international system, and even of attributing to such abstractions the behavioral characters of flesh-and-blood human beings. We observed, finally, that such usage of ecological terms and modes of speaking seemed to add significant moral and civic as well as purely intellectual overtones and nuances to political discourse.

These observations suggested the need for a fresh look at ecological concepts and theories, both in general and in the particular context of political actions and relationships. Our purpose was not to offer still another approach or scheme for studying political phenomena. It has been rather to clarify and to straighten out, if possible, certain semantic (and inferentially, intellectual) issues that tend to bedevil all approaches to the study of human affairs.

Our point of departure was the term *environment*. This term is widely and loosely used in discussions of human affairs. Environment (or *milieu,* the term we prefer for general reference) connotes some idea of relationship, both in popular usage and in the technical discourse of the special fields from which ecological concepts and theories mainly come—in particular, certain branches of biology, psychology, and geography. In ecological parlance, something is conceived to be surrounded, or encompassed—that is to say, environed—by something else in some sense that is deemed significant. The organizing concepts are thus *milieu* and *environed unit,* and ecological theory is concerned mainly with *relationships* between them.

These relationships have been conceived in various ways. The older modes—environmental determinism (reviewed in Chapter 3) and its watered-down derivative, free-will environmentalism (Chapter 4)—generally carried strong teleological overtones and nuances, and did not differentiate between man-milieu relationships derived from cognition and those otherwise derived. Revolt against determinism and environmentalism evoked the possibilistic mode of viewing man-milieu relationships, a mode associated in America with the philosophical doctrine of pragmatism (Chapter 5). In a possibilistic analysis, the actor's values and preferences, moods and attitudes, purposes and intentions are bypassed altogether. His decisions (undertakings, strategies) are taken as *givens* without psychological explication, a point often missed or muddied in theoretical discussions of possibilism. A possibilistic analysis yields either an explanation or a prediction of the outcome of a *given* undertaking, actual or postulated. Such an analysis is thus directed to the issue of the actor's capabilities with reference to the *given* undertaking. In order to bring in questions of motivation, intent, choice, and mode of making decisions, students of human affairs have relied heavily on intuitive explanation, often called "empathetic understanding," supplemented by more formal "dispositional models"—that is, probabilistic models of typical or normally expectable behavior (Chapter 6). In recent years, various conceptual schemes have provided more systematic frameworks for empirical research into the processes of decision-making, especially decision-making in complex organizational settings (Chapter 7). With reference both to decisions (undertakings) and to the outcomes or operational results thereof, the concepts of necessary and sufficient conditions, and other features of more general theories of explanation, have helped to put into sharper focus the issues involved in ascertaining and interpreting man-milieu relationships (as indicated in Chapters 8 and 9).

Ecological concepts and theories have evolved chiefly within frames of discourse concerned with living organisms. In those contexts, environed units are invariably concrete entities locatable in space. Ecological concepts and theories have been adapted for application to the analysis of human groups conceived as aggregates of concrete individuals. Also, as indicated in Chapter 2, one finds these terms and modes of expression increasingly used with reference to abstract entities, called social systems, locatable in space only indirectly and by derivation.

Neither milieu nor environed unit can be defined without reference to the other. This is so because, ecologically speaking, there is no concept of milieu in general—in a vacuum, so to speak. A milieu is invariably the milieu of some specified environed unit. No two units are environed by exactly the same milieu, since no two units occupy exactly the same space or are responsive to exactly the same set of limiting factors. What is included in a particular milieu depends on how the environed unit is defined. The ultimate building blocks of all theories of man-milieu relationships are obviously concrete human individuals— a specified artist, farmer, businessman, athlete, statesman, or other. It is easy, though not very precise, to extend the concept of environed unit to a concrete human aggregate, especially when that aggregate exhibits the homogeneity of a group or the features of a more formal organization. But when a concrete human group is metamorphosed into such abstractions as corporation, state, political system, and international system, methodological puzzles and difficulties emerge. In general, as previously argued, these tend to be more troublesome in the analysis of psychological behavior than in the analysis of achievements.

When the environed unit is a human organism, both human species heredity and genetic variations among individuals may be relevant to explanations of behavior and achievements. Now there is manifestly no identity, or even close parallel, between an organism's genetically derived characters and the structures, or patterns, of a social group, organization, or system. It would be purely metaphorical to attribute genetic characters to such entities. But a social organization, or system, may exhibit subpatterns, or substructures; and such substructures may affect the operation of the system as a whole. For example, institutions of government, and social rules governing who does what within a society, may be viewed as social structures which may affect both the policies and the capabilities of a national community as a whole.

It is a truism that social structures change through time. It is likewise evident that such changes may entail important consequences, political or other. Many examples come to mind. The Czarist imperial system was transmuted by revolution into the Soviet political system. To cite another example, the historic multipolar international system was transmuted briefly into a loose bipolar system, and now seems to be in process of further transformation towards a complex pattern exhibiting both bipolarity and polycentricity.

We noted, with reference to individual persons, that it is often impossible to differentiate cleanly between genetic and environmental limitations. The same can be said of differentiating limitations derived from an organization's substructures and from the milieu in which the organization operates. In the latter case, as in the former, both the structures of the unit and the factors of its milieu may be significantly relevant to explaining or predicting decisions (undertakings, strategies, policies)—but with this essential difference: In the case of the social organization, or system, the only entities psychologically capable of making decisions are human individuals who appear, from the perspective of the system as a whole, to be substructures of the system. Troublesome ecological difficulties arise when the psychological behavior of the system's human agents is attributed to the system *qua* system.

In Chapter 2 we asked some blunt questions regarding efforts to bend ecological concepts and theories into the mold of general behavior systems theory. We repeat some of those questions here: In what sense can a system, conceived as an abstract entity (derived but analytically distinct from concrete social structures) be said to have a mlieu? What is surrounded, or encompassed, or environed? In what sense? Spatial? Purely metaphorical? What instrumental mechanisms and processes connect such an abstract entity and its imputed milieu? Are these psychological, in toto or in part? An affirmative answer to this last question poses a very refractory methodological difficulty, previously discussed and to which we now briefly return.

If we say, for example, that insularity has *influenced* the foreign policy of Great Britain, we are saying no more and no less than that through some period of time those persons who have made decisions in the name of the British state have *perceived* that their country is an island, and have *reacted psychologically* in specified ways to that image. If we say that Hitler's invasion of Poland was the immediate cause of Britain's entry into World War II, we are asserting precisely the same kind of connection. Whether the factor asserted to be causal is a feature of the nonhuman environment or an event in the social milieu, the linkage is the same. That is to say, it is psychological, and no other. So too are the concepts that identify and the theories that purport to account for every aspect of the decision-making process: the statesman's schedule of values and preferences, his moods and attitudes, his motives and intentions, his cognition and recognition, his modes of framing alternatives and of deciding among them. The position, we repeat, is that environing conditions and events can affect decisions (and hence undertakings, strategies, and policies) *only* by being perceived and reacted to *psychologically* in the light of the environed individual's felt needs and previous experience.

What an individual perceives and how he reacts to it

THE ISSUES REVIEWED

(that is, the composition of his psycho-milieu) may or may not correspond closely to his operational milieu, the complex of conditions and events that will determine the outcome of whatever he decides to undertake. He may react imaginatively or stupidly, rationally or irrationally, to what he perceives. But it is his percepts and reactions thereto, not the milieu as it is, or as someone else apperceives it, that determines what is to be undertaken.

A corollary of this conclusion and its supporting argument is that *psycho*-ecological concepts and theories are relevant only with reference to entities capable of experiencing needs, formulating problems, perceiving phenomena by seeing, hearing, and other sensory behavior. Social organizations do not exhibit these properties, apart from the flesh-and-blood human beings who comprise them. For this reason, the analogical extension of *psycho*-ecological terms and relational ideas to such abstractions as the state, the political system, or the international system seems to us more likely to muddy than to clarify one's understanding of the undertakings, strategies, and policies from which the patterns of international politics are derived.

For this reason, as previously emphasized in Chapter 2, some of the analogies and imagery of general behavior systems theories pose troublesome issues. We have queried, for example, Kaplan's thesis that "if . . . the specific action content is removed and they are treated in terms of the routing of information within the system, the various psychological mechanisms are isomorphic with mechanisms manifested in the behavior of social organizations." [1]

We find even more confusing his assertions that "a *social system* is *motivated* as truly as an individual hu-

[1] M. A. Kaplan, *System and Process in International Politics*, Wiley, 1957, p. 253.

man being"; that "the *choice* the *system makes* determines . . . ," etc.; and that "the environment will be redefined in terms which permit the *system* to *scan* for the information *it perceives* to be relevant to the *choices it has made*." Furthermore, in what sense is Kaplan speaking when he characterizes the "pathology" of social systems in terms of such psychological concepts as "catharsis," "cathexis," "compulsive and psychopathic syndromes," "schizoid and paranoid syndromes," "manic and depressive syndromes," and the like? (italics added)[2]

Some systems theorists explicitly introduce the "organismic" concept (reminiscent of Hegelian doctrine) into their discussions of the state and the international system.[8] But we know of none who claim that any political system exhibits structures isomorphic to the eyes, ears, nose, mouth, brain, and other sensory structures of the human organism. We recognize that most systems theorists would stop far short of claiming that social and biological structures and functions are isomorphic in any but a purely metaphorical sense. But the issue remains whether one derives clearer and richer insight into the operations of political organizations by endowing them even metaphorically with pseudo-biological structures and pseudo-psychological functions.

Deutsch meets this issue with the following argument: "The new experiences and notions ["of control processes, memory, and learning"] promise to replace the classic ana-

[2] *Ibid.*, pp. 254ff.

[8] For example, C. A. McClelland, "Applications of General Systems Theory in International Relations," in J. N. Rosenau *et al., International Politics and Foreign Policy,* Free Press, 1961, pp. 412ff. On the reference to Hegel, see R. C. Buck, "On the Logic of General Behavior Systems Theory," in *The Foundations of Science and the Concepts of Psychology and Psychoanalysis,* edited by H. Feigl and M. Scriven, Minnesota Studies in the Philosophy of Science, v. 1, University of Minnesota Press, 1956, p. 224.

logues or models of mechanism, organism, and process, which so long have dominated so much of scientific thinking. . . . In the place of these obsolescent models, we now have an array of self-controlling machines that react to their environment, as well as to the results of their own behavior; that store, process, and apply information; and that have, in some cases, a limited capacity to learn."

With reference both to mechanical and to social systems, Deutsch speaks of the *system*'s "environment," and the "behavior" of the *system*. He is manifestly aware that such rhetoric may be misleading. He explicitly warns that the operations of machines (electronic computers, for example) and of social organizations are not "*thought in the human sense,*" and that he is merely speaking in analogies and parallels.[4]

Heuristic as these parallels undoubtedly are, one may still enter a gentle protest against such use of psycho-ecological terms and ideas. Reminders that machines and social systems do not think in a "human sense" seems unlikely to deter most people from reacting to such rhetoric in precisely that sense. That is to say, the *human* connotations of such terms as "behavior," "actor," "action," and "environment" are deeply rooted in our culture, perhaps too deeply rooted to be eradicated by any number of verbal warnings.

We have previously noted some of the consequences entailed in such usage of psycho-ecological terms and modes of expression. It tends to reify abstractions and to divert attention from the human persons who ultimately decide what is to be undertaken. In the case of the state, reification buttresses ethnocentric values and images which characterize so much of the discussion of

[4] K. W. Deutsch, *The Nerves of Government,* Free Press, 1963, pp. 79-80.

foreign policy, military defense, and international politics in general.

A byproduct of such usage of psycho-ecological terms and concepts is the implication that the system runs autonomously, out of control of the human persons who alone are capable of scheduling values, perceiving and reacting to conditions and events, formulating projects and making decisions. As Stanley Hoffmann has cogently put it: "International systems [and this applies to national political systems, too] are discussed as if they had a compulsive will of their own. . . . Each system assigns roles to actors; the structure of the system sets its needs, its needs determine its objective, and [quoting Kaplan] 'the objectives of a system are values for the system.' " [5]

This criticism, so far as we are concerned, is not to be construed as an attack on the system-perspective or on all aspects of system theories.[6] Our argument goes rather to the imperative need for re-examining the vocabulary used to describe the operations of political systems *qua* systems. Specifically (to re-emphasize a suggestion offered in Chapter 2), a vocabulary is needed that avoids ascription of psycho-ecological behavior to abstract entities, or at least minimizes such ascription as much as possible.

This is not especially difficult to achieve. One can cite numerous examples in which political systems are described and generalized with minimal use of psycho-ecological rhetoric.[7] We have previously noted, in particu-

[5] Stanley Hoffmann, "International Relations: The Long Road to Theory," in *World Politics,* 1959, v. 11, p. 360.
[6] There are semantic and logical grounds for attacking much of the theorizing about social systems. For such a critique, see R. C. Buck, "On the Logic of General Behavior Systems Theory," cited earlier in this chapter.
[7] For example, R. D. Masters, "A Multi-Bloc Model of the International System," in *American Political Science Review,* 1961, v. 55, pp. 780*ff;* also K. W. Deutsch and J. D. Singer, "Multipolar

lar, Quincy Wright's substitution of "geographic and analytical fields" in place of environment, in his scheme for
analyzing the international system." [8] The geographer
S. B. Jones has deployed somewhat similar concepts in his
"Unified Field Theory of Political Geography." [9] The particular solutions just cited may or may not be the best that
can be contrived. But they do confirm that political systems can be described and generalized in other than psycho-ecological terms.

Despite the ambiguities and other consequences of
using psycho-ecological terms and concepts with reference
to states and other social systems, it seems likely that
such usage will continue. On that assumption, one can
only urge that the referents of such terms be kept as concrete as possible. At the very least, the rhetoric employed
should direct attention to the human agent or agents of
the system, who alone are psychologically capable of the
behavior attributed to the system *qua* system.

When the analytic focus is shifted from psychological
behavior (decisions, undertakings, strategies, policies) to
the operational results of decisions (outcomes, achievements, capabilities for achievement, relational patterns derived from interaction), the methodological difficulties
reviewed and re-emphasized above either disappear or at
least become less troublesome. For reasons previously
stressed, the concept of environed unit is generally easier to handle, and manipulation entails less risk of intellectual confusion, when the problem is to estimate opportunities and limitations latent in the milieu and in

Power Systems and International Stability," in *World Politics*, 1964,
v. 16, pp. 390*ff*. Many other examples could be cited.

[8] Quincy Wright, *The Study of International Relations*, Appleton-
Century-Crofts, 1954, ch. 32.

[9] *Annals*, Association of American Geographers, 1954, v. 44, pp.
111*ff;* reprinted in W. A. D. Jackson *et al., Politics and Geographic
Relationships*, Prentice-Hall, 1964, pp. 101*ff*.

the structures of the environed unit, with reference to some *given* course of action, and some *given* frame of operational contingencies, than when the problem is to explain or to predict how the system itself functions with reference to formulating and implementing a course of action.

As shown in Chapters 8 and 9, such an analysis may be addressed to either an historical or a future state of affairs. In the former context, the question is: How was it possible for the result to occur that did in fact occur? In predictive contexts, the question becomes: *Given* some decision, or strategy of action, and *given also* a postulated operational contingency or situation, what outcomes are possible, and what is the order of probability among them?

As indicated in Chapter 5, such an analysis may yield an explanation or a prediction with reference either to a single specified undertaking or to a more complex set of actions and interactions. In either case, the analysis of results or outcomes involves identifying and evaluating both those structures of the environed unit and those factors of its milieu *that set limits to performance*. This, we repeat, is the essence of political capabilities analysis, first developeed with special reference to military operations, and more recently expanded to include all the styles and techniques of international statecraft.

One can carry out a capabilities analysis with reference to any operational unit: an individual person, a concrete group, or a complex organization, such as an athletic team, a business firm, an army, an organized political community as a whole, or any other. Whereas it is difficult, if not utterly impossible, to investigate decision-making and other psychological behavior without going to the level of specific human persons who make decisions on behalf of the organization, the analytical situation is quite different when it comes to explaining or predicting capabilities: that is, achievements, actual or potential, with reference to a *given* undertaking or strategy. It is generally easier, for obvious reasons, to estimate the capabilities of a relatively simple concrete unit (for example, an individual person) than of a complex social organization, or "system" (such as a business firm, or a state). But one can usually make many kinds of enlightening statements about the capabilities of the most complex social systems without investigating decision-making or other psychological behavior. This is so, we repeat, because every capabilities analysis takes off from a *given undertaking* or set of undertakings, actual or postulated. Otherwise there could be no achievements, and hence no capabilities to analyze.

Take, for example, the case of a concert pianist. Until he decides to play something and then plays it, the music critic has nothing to write about. The same holds for a farm, or an athletic team, or an army, or any other organization. As previously noted, one can say many meaningful things about the performance of a football team, without investigating the psychological behavior of the quarterback or whoever calls the plays. One can compare the skills and styles of play of the opposing teams: the ball handling, blocking, tackling, rushing, etc. But the moment one asks questions regarding the strategy of the game—why a particular sequence of plays was called rather than some other—one has to go to the level of the particular person who decided what plays to call.

Suppose the problem is to investigate the operation of a farm. In order to answer the question: "Why did the farmer plant wheat instead of corn or some other crop?" one has to investigate empirically the particular farmer's particular decision-making (as described in Chapter 7), or else invoke some probabilistic psychological model of typical or normally expectable farmer-behavior (as in

Chapter 6). In either case, the analysis is at the concrete human-actor level. On the other hand, with reference to a *given* layout of crops (representing specified initial decisions), one can formulate numerous significant statements about outcomes (that is, about the capabilities of the farm) without further attention to initial decisions. For example, one might come to the conclusion that the given choice of crops represents low or high risk of failure because of conditions of soil, expectable weather, state of the market, etc.[10]

Similarly, it is possible to make significant statements regarding the political relations of states without identifying and investigating the specific psychological behaviors of specified human agents of the states under consideration. But one can do so *only within some frame of* GIVEN *data or assumptions* with regard to policies (what is to be undertaken) and operational contingencies (against whom and under what conditions).

The purpose of such an analysis may be to estimate the international political capabilities of a particular state; or the analysis may focus on the larger patterns of power and influence (what we prefer to call political potential) among units of the society of nations. In historical cases such an analysis may be directed to the question: How was it possible for State A to wield the power, or to exert the influence, or to play the international role that it did in fact achieve (a mode of analysis described in Chapter 8)? In a predictive context the analysis may be designed to yield an estimate of the power that A could

[10] It might be contended that one reason for the apparent success of theorizing in economics is because economists have focussed mainly on outcomes (capabilities) within a frame of relatively simple *assumptions* regarding motivation and strategy. Whenever they have ventured far outside the classic model of "economic man," they have encountered the same difficulties that beset the analysis of political decision-making.

wield, or the influence it could exert, or the role it could play in a postulated future frame of strategy and operating conditions (as in Chapter 9). Or the analysis may yield broader generalizations (sometimes called geopolitical hypotheses) that purport to explain or to predict global or regional patterns of political interaction and relationships.

It is a truism (though one too often neglected) that conclusions regarding the international capabilities of states are always comparative. This comparative aspect is covered by the expression "operational contingencies." That is to say, what one state can achieve depends both on what is undertaken, and on the location, operational characteristics, and policies of other states, and on the overall configuration of political relationships in the society of nations. There is no sensible concept of capabilities in the abstract—in a vacuum, so to speak. From the ecological perspective, the policies, resources, location, and operational characteristics of other states are simply ingredients of the milieu of the state whose capabilities are being estimated.

Without some set of *given* undertakings (strategies, policies), actual or postulated, with reference to some frame of operational contingencies, actual or postulated, there can be no estimation of political capabilities, and no analysis of international relational patterns. For example, one cannot speak sensibly about the capabilities of Communist China without laying down some frame of assumptions as to what China's rulers will be trying to accomplish, against what adversaries, by what means, with what assistance, in what places, over what time-span, etc. Failure to keep discussions of capabilities and international patterns within some such policy-contingency frame of reference is all too common. Such failure tends to reduce statements about the "elements" or "foundations" of a given state's power and influence to vacuous ir-relevancies. The data of physical geography, or of demography, or of economic production, or of any other field have no intrinsic political relevance whatever. Such data acquire political relevance and significance only when related to some frame of assumptions as to what is to be undertaken or attempted in what operational contingencies.

The preceding sentence, it should be clearly understood, refers only to the estimation of capabilities, and the explanation or prediction of international political patterns. If the task is to explain how certain strategies or policies came to be adopted, or to predict what State *A*'s human agents are likely to undertake, different criteria of relevance and significance are involved (as reviewed earlier in this chapter, and discussed at length in previous chapters). The point here is simply that one cannot estimate capabilities in the absence of some frame of *given* specified strategies and operational contingencies, actual or postulated. In the absence of these *givens*, inventories of environmental data have no more intrinsic political significance than so much blowing sand or drifting snow.

In arguing this conclusion we are not unmindful of the multifaceted operations of general intelligence-gathering organizations such as the Central Intelligence Agency. It may be economical for the governments of Great Powers, concerned simultaneously with many international problems and transactions, to collect inventories of data on a very broad front, without specific reference in every instance to particular envisaged needs. But such practice should not obscure the essential and indisputable conclusion that data acquire political significance only within some frame of questions to be answered. Moreover, despite superficial appearances to the contrary, it could probably be established that particular envisaged needs, with reference to ongoing or anticipated problems, do largely affect the operations of multipurpose intelligence agencies.[11]

The policy-contingency frame of reference may be short-term and more or less specific. For example, what factors may set limits to realization of the declared Russian intention to overtake the economic lead of the United States by some specified date? What factors may affect execution of the declared French policy to acquire a credible independent system of nuclear weapons? What factors may affect the outcome of the British Government's declared intention to stabilize Britain's international balance of payments?

Such relatively short-term and rather specific policy-contingency *givens* shade off into longer-term and more general questions, in which policy-contingency assumptions are latent rather than specified. For example, a few years ago, the geographer G. E. Cressey devoted a whole book to arguing the thesis that, for geographic reasons, the Soviet Union could never "achieve strictly first-class

[11] A superficial reading of K. W. Deutsch's essay, "Toward an Inventory of Basic Trends and Patterns in Comparative and International Politics" (*American Political Science Review*, 1960, v. 54, pp. 34ff), might lead one to infer that Deutsch is arguing implicitly for the intrinsic political relevance of assorted categories of data: geographic, economic, demographic, etc. More careful reading, however, especially of the section in which he discusses the process of building and verifying hypotheses, leads us to the conclusion that he does recognize (at least implicitly) that inventories of data acquire political significance only in the context of *given* policies and/or operational contingencies, actual or postulated. Another essay on capabilities analysis, in which the essentiality of such assumptions is made quite explicit, is "The Power Inventory and National Strategy," by S. B. Jones, in *World Politics*, 1954, v. 6, pp. 421ff. Our own earlier work, *Foundations of National Power* (especially the first edition, Princeton University Press, 1945), is an exhibit of failure to link with sufficient clarity the discussion of so-called power factors to a policy-contingency frame of reference.

rank" in international politics. Yet nowhere in the book
did he specify what "first-class rank" might involve in
terms of policies and operational contingencies.[12]

In another classic example, the British geographer Sir
Halford Mackinder asserted that "the grouping of lands
and seas, and of fertility and natural pathways, is such
as to lead to the growth of empires, and in the end of a
single world empire." This thesis, especially when read in
the context in which it was propounded, comes closer to
articulating a policy-contingency frame of reference. It is
evident that Mackinder assumed implicitly: (a) that Great
Powers expand to the limit of their capabilities, and (b)
that this limit is ultimately determined by the test of
large-scale war with other Great Powers.[13]

This particular policy-contingency frame underlies virtually all past discussions of international politics. It has
long pervaded the writings of journalists and scholars as
well as the actions of statesmen. It is especially evident
in references to the "Great Powers." In the words of *The
Economist,* "A Great Power is a country capable of
waging active and autonomous war against another Great
Power." [14] Still more generally, Spykman asserted that
the power of a state is "in the last instance the power to
wage war." [15] This theme recurs in nearly all textbooks
and treatises on international politics. As long as military
war, however brutal and demoralizing, remained an
effective and acceptable means of supporting a government's policies, such wars provided a rough-and-ready

[12] G. E. Cressey, *How Strong Is Russia?,* Syracuse University
Press, 1954.

[13] H. J. Mackinder, *Democratic Ideals and Reality,* Holt, 1919;
reprinted in 1942.

[14] "What Is a Great Power?" in *The Economist,* March 11, 1944,
p. 331.

[15] N. J. Spykman, *America's Strategy in World Politics,* Har-
court, 1942, pp. 18-19.

yardstick for ranking nations in a hierarchy of power, "like the chickens studied by biologists, which are found to have a definite pecking order when a feed pan is set down among them." [16]

This conception of international politics has colored all past theorizing and speculation regarding the geographical distribution of political potential in the society of nations. Many geopolitical hypotheses have been propounded: hypotheses that purport to identify those factors, the uneven distribution of which over the face of the earth has determined (or presumably will determine) the major patterns of international politics. For Mahan, Mackinder, and others, the determinative set of environing factors was mainly, though never exclusively, the layout and configuration of the lands and seas of the globe. For Ellsworth Huntington, and others before and after him, the strategic political variable has been climate. Still others have discovered the key to the rise and decline of nations, and the geographical patterns of international politics, in the uneven distribution of "natural resources," or in the uneven distribution and differential growth-rates of national populations, or in national differences in economic development and technological proficiency, or in some other set of variables. So far as we can ascertain, all such geopolitical hypotheses represent estimations of the relative capabilities of nations, derived by possibilistic reasoning, within a policy-contingency framework of competitive expansion and periodic payoffs by means of large-scale military war.[17]

Until quite recently nearly all students of international

[16] W. F. Ogburn *et al.*, *Technology and International Relations*, University of Chicago Press, 1949, p. 1.

[17] For further discussion of this thesis, see our "Geopolitical Hypotheses in Technological Perspective," in *World Politics*, 1963, v. 15, pp. 187*ff*.

politics would have accepted this "realist" frame of expansion and recurrent military war as the basis for analyzing the relative capabilities and achievements from which
international patterns are deduced. It admittedly was difficult to compare and rank states in a hierarchy of power
even in the days when periodic major wars provided a
crude sort of objective testing of assumptions and judgments. Even then, as indicated above, there was always
disagreement as to which variables were most significant.
The development of weapons systems that cast doubt on
the possibility of meaningful victory for anyone in the
contingency of World War III adds further complicating
dimensions to the concept of international capabilities.
It is manifestly more difficult to rank states according to
their total impacts on other nations when many nonmili-
tary and paramilitary variables have to be given more
weight, and when all the variables are changing more
rapidly than formerly, and at different rates in different
countries.[18]

This state of affairs has evoked numerous assertions that
the estimation of political capabilities has become a hope-
lessly unmanageable problem. A characteristic expression
of this pessimism comes from the pen of Walter Millis:
"There may have been a time when it was reasonable to
estimate national power in terms of mobilizable military
establishments, and to conclude that, short of actual war,
the nation with the biggest battalions was most likely to

[18] In the early days of the nuclear age, a British analyst,
Maurice Ash, devised a scheme for answering the question: "What
determines, at a given moment, the exact amount of force that one
state is exerting upon another?" In presenting his scheme, he contended that "any analysis of power, of the forces of coercion, of
politics, which cannot answer or attempt to answer this question
must abandon all pretensions to being scientific and be recognized
as, in fact, purely speculative." "An Analysis of Power, with Special
Reference to International Politics," in *World Politics*, 1951, v. 3,
pp. 218ff.

· 220 ·

have its way in diplomatic maneuver and negotiation."
But today, he continues, "national power . . . is a resultant of many incommensurable factors, of which mobilizable military power is only one, and even that one
not easily measured in practice. In addition, it is necessary to include the factors of human and raw material resources, geographic and strategic position, productivity
of industrial plant, the stage of technology, domestic unity
and morale, the firmness of the alliance systems, the effec-
tiveness of statecraft and propaganda, the intangibles of
'prestige.' " All these variables, he laments, "are not merely
incommensurable; it is difficult to compare their values
as between one [political] system and another, while all
the values shift in accord with the specific situations which
arise and even in accordance with one's concept of war." [19]
    The necessity as well as the increasing complexity of
setting a capabilities analysis within a policy-contingency
framework is easily illustrated. Suppose one undertakes
to compare the international capabilities of the United
States and the Soviet Union. Suppose, further, that one
considers this problem in the light of three different policy-
contingency assumptions: (1) that the Soviet and American governments will sooner or later resort to total nuclear war; (2) that the cold war, accompanied by competitive armament development but no large-scale military combat, will continue indefinitely; and (3) that the
growth of Chinese power and influence, accompanied by
progressive erosion of both the Communist and the anti-
Communist coalitions, will foster in Moscow and in Washington a growing felt need for closer and less antagonistic
relations during the next decade or so.
    Is it not immediately apparent that the particular "ca-
pabilities" that might be decisive in fighting a nuclear

[19] Walter Millis, "U.S.—Balance of Power—U.S.S.R.," in *New
York Times Magazine*, August 2, 1959.

THE ISSUES REVIEWED

war may differ radically from those required for indefinite cold war? And that the qualities required for either may be quite different from those required to negotiate and carry on an acceptable détente?

Numerous frames of analysis have been offered for estimating and comparing the capabilities of states under various policy-contingency assumptions. In another place we have suggested one possible approach to this complex set of issues.[20] The essence of our suggestion was to compare national capabilities under the functional categories of: (1) information-providing functions, (2) information-utilizing functions, (3) means-providing functions, (4) means-utilizing functions, and (5) resistance functions, to the extent that these last are not covered in the preceding four categories.

This may or may not prove to be an especially fruitful approach. We cite it here chiefly because it directs attention once again to the essential difference between a policy analysis and a capabilities analysis. Categories (1) and (2) represent aspects of decision-making. But these and other aspects of decision-making enter into the estimation of capabilities in a context wholly different from the context of explanation or prediction of particular decisions. In the latter type of analysis, one endeavors to ascertain how those who make decisions in the name of the state envisage the opportunities and limitations implicit in their milieu. Such an inquiry is *not* capability analysis, but is rather an aspect of policy analysis (as was shown more specifically in Chapters 6 and 7, and re-examined in Chapters 8 and 9. Investigation of aspects of decision-making enters into capabilities analysis only when the purpose of the analyst is *not* to explain how a particular decision came to be taken, or to

[20] See H. and M. Sprout, *Foundations of International Politics*, Van Nostrand, 1962, pp. 167ff.

· 222 ·

predict what decision is likely to be taken in specified contingencies, *but rather* when the analyst's purpose is to reach an *independent qualitative judgment* as to how a government's decision-making processes affect its level of achievement or quality of performance.

Putting a capabilities problem into some policy-contingency frame of reference, and setting up a scheme for breaking down the problem into some set of functions to be evaluated, constitute only the initial steps in the estimation of political capabilities. Given the most explicit assumptions (as to what is to be undertaken, by what means, against what adversaries, when and where, etc.) and given the most elegant conceptual scheme for analytically differentiating significant functional aspects of a state's capabilities, one still has to establish criteria for judging the significance of variables: for example, the international significance, if any, of geographic location, distance, space, and configuration, the uneven distribution of natural resources and population, variations in economic development, political organization, and other social phenomena. In short, one learns nothing about the relative capabilities of nations merely by collecting, sorting, and comparing raw data. Such data acquire political significance, we repeat, in one way, and one way only: by application of suitable explanatory hypotheses, as described and illustrated in Chapters 8 and 9.

We cannot take these issues further here. If anyone is disappointed because we have concentrated on semantic and conceptual issues and given little attention to particular substantive problems, we can only reply that clarification and assessment of the former were the task that we undertook. The ecological perspective and ecological ideas permeate political discourse, just as they do every other sector of human activity. But ecological terms are often used loosely and imprecisely, and ecological relationships are asserted without regard to, probably often without awareness of, the intellectual and other consequences that particular modes of expression may entail.

As emphasized from the outset, a necessary first step towards clearer understanding of man-milieu relationships is to distinguish relationships derived via psychological processes from those derived otherwise. With respect to the former, the thesis is that (with a possible exception dealt with in Chapter 3) values and preferences, moods and attitudes, choices and decisions are relatable to the milieu only via the environed individual's selective perception and his psychological reactions to what is perceived. From the perspective of decisions and decision-making, what matters is how the individual or group imagines the milieu to be, *not* how it actually is. A corollary of this thesis is that *only* psycho-ecological concepts and theories are relevant to descriptions and explanations of decisions (policies, strategies, undertakings), but that psychological concepts and theories are appropriately applicable *only* to environed units capable of psychological behavior.

In the context of human affairs, this corollary confines the relevance of psycho-ecological concepts and theories to human individuals, concrete human groups, and to more formal organizations *in their concrete human aspect*. We have argued, and we reiterate again, that *psycho*-ecological terms and modes of expression cannot be sensibly employed with reference to high-level abstractions such as the state and the international system, *unless* it is made explicitly clear that the reference is not to the system, *qua* system, but *only* to the human agents of the system. Avoidance of words and sentences that attribute human-like characters to the state, *qua* state, and to the international system, *qua* system, is, in our view, a long overdue step towards combating the tendency to reification that, paradoxically, dehumanizes politics, a tendency that also fosters deterministic thinking about political institutions and relationships. Alternative vocabularies are needed and are readily available.

With respect to the operational results of decisions, our thesis is that what matters is how the milieu actually is, *not* how the environed individual or group imagines it to be. In every instance, the structures of the environed unit and the factors of the milieu set limits to that unit's achievement, with reference to whatever task or strategy is undertaken. From the standpoint of achievement, at least some of these limiting factors may be effective, irrespective of whether or how the environed individual or group perceived and took them into account in defining the undertaking and setting the course of action.

A corollary of this thesis is that explanations of achievement and estimations of capabilities for achievement invariably and necessarily presuppose antecedent undertakings or assumptions regarding undertakings. Unless there is an undertaking, there can be no achievement— and nothing to explain or to estimate. This requirement is implicit in all possibilistic analyses, of which estimation of the capabilities of states and explanation of international political patterns are simply special cases.

We say special cases because, as previously emphasized, the ecological perspective permeates every sector of human activity. More general awareness of the intellectual, and also the moral and civic, consequences of ecological terms, modes of expression, and theories of man-milieu relationships should contribute to more precise and enlightening explanations and predictions of human behavior and achievement.

INDEX

action defined, 23
adaptation as ecological concept, 25
Alger, C. F., concept of system environment, 6, 41n
Allport, Floyd, on state personification, 36n
analogical extension of concepts and theories, 16f, 205ff
analogies, uses of in hypothesis formation, 150
apperception, 28, 120; semantic aspect, 46n
areal differences in environmental opportunities, 89
areal differentiation, as organizing concept of geography, 13f
Ash, M. M., concept of political power, 21; military basis of power in international politics, 220

Bailey, T. A., on geographic basis of American isolationism, 59
Barker, R. G., on perceptive basis of behavior, 132
Barrows, H. H., on ecological perspective in geography, 7; on nature of geographic discipline, 102n
behavior, defined, 23; explanation of purposeful, 170ff; see also empathetic understanding, dispositional model, psychological theories
behavioral models, elements of, 101

behavioral theory, ecological aspects of, 8; see also psychological theories
Blount, B. K., on geographic distribution of geniuses, 32
Blum, H. F., on genetic and environmental aspects of behavior, 32n
Bowman, Isaiah, on cost as an environmental limitation, 87; on manipulative connotations of possibilism, 85
Bronowski, Jacob, on explanation, 148n; on probabilistic aspect of prediction, 176
Brown, Robert, on explanations in social science, 144n
Bruck, H. W., see Snyder, R. C.
Brunswick, Egon, on image and reality, 139n; on probabilistic nature of prediction, 176
Buck, R. C., critique of systems theory, 208n, 210n
Buckle, H. T., use of deterministic rhetoric, 50
Burns, A. L., on relevance of behavioral sciences to analysis of international system, 40

Caesar, A. A. L., on cultural lag as factor in geographic analysis, 110
Cambon, Jules, on geographic "influences" on French foreign policy, 74
capabilities, concept of, 11, 168; political applications, 98, 222
capabilities analysis, salient characteristics of, 211f; policy–contingency basis of,

environmental bases of, 219; policy–contingency assumptions implicit in, 219*f*

Gestalt theory, 130; *see also* psycho-milieu

Glacken, C. L., on technology and environmental control, 53; on origin of possibilism, 86*n*

Great Power, concept of, 218

Grunberg, E. and Modigliani, F., on social effects of public predictions, 183*n*

Hartshorne, Richard, on usage of environmental terms, 28*n;* on environmentalism, 79*n;* on origin of possibilism, 84*n;* on nature of geographic discipline, 102*n*

Hawley, A. H., on concept of environment, 26

Helmer, O., and Resher, N., on function of experts, 193

Hempel, C. G., on theory of historical explanation, 145*f;* 156*n;* on "empathetic understanding" in historiography, 170*f;* on logical structure of explanation and prediction, 177*n*

heredity and environment, 27

historical explanations, modes of testing, 168

Hoar, G. F., geographical misconception of the Pacific Ocean, 126*n*

Hoffmann, Stanley, on deterministic connotations of systems theory, 210

Hofstadter, Richard, on pragmatism and possibilism, 84*f*

homeostasis, deterministic connotation of, 64*f*

"how possible" question in explanation theory, 157; possibilistic model of analysis, 168*f*

Huntington, Ellsworth, climatic interpretation of history, 54*f*

hypothesis, variant usage of term, 47*n*

image-reality discongruities, sources of, 127*ff*

influence, concept of, 21, 77; as psychological interaction, 206

interaction, defined, 24

international politics, defined, 19; environmental ideas in textbooks, 5

James, P. E., on nature of geography, 13; on image and reality, 131*n*

James, William, contribution to possibilism, 85

Jones, Emrys, on variant concepts of causality, 67*n;* on explanation in geographic analysis, 142; on acceptable explanations, 151*n*, 153*f*

Jones, S. B., on "field" concept for geographic analysis, 211; on capabilities analysis, 217*n*

Kaplan, M. A., on isomorphism of biological entities and social systems, 35, 207

Kirk, William, on relevance of *Gestalt* theory for geographic analysis, 130*f*

Koffka, Kurt, on discongruities between image and reality, 122*n*

Latham, George, on cost as aspect of possibilism, 87

LeBon, J. H., on concept of environment, 26

Levy, M. J., Jr., on functional

Other books published for
The Center of International Studies
Woodrow Wilson School of Public and International
Affairs

Gabriel A. Almond, *The Appeals of Communism*
Gabriel A. Almond and James S. Coleman, editors, *The Politics of the Developing Areas*
Gabriel A. Almond and Sidney Verba, *The Civic Culture: Political Attitudes and Democracy in Five Nations*
Richard J. Barnet and Richard A. Falk, *Security in Disarmament*
Cyril E. Black and Thomas P. Thornton, editors, *Communism and Revolution: The Strategic Uses of Political Violence*
Robert J. C. Butow, *Tojo and the Coming of the War*
Miriam Camps, *Britain and the European Community, 1955-1963*
Bernard C. Cohen, *The Political Process and Foreign Policy: The Making of the Japanese Peace Settlement*
Bernard C. Cohen, *The Press and Foreign Policy*
Charles De Visscher, *Theory and Reality in Public International Law*, translated by P. E. Corbett
Frederick S. Dunn, *Peace-making and the settlement with Japan*
Herman Kahn, *On Thermonuclear War*
W. W. Kaufmann, editor, *Military Policy and National Security*
Klaus Knorr, *The War Potential of Nations*
Klaus Knorr, editor, *NATO and American Security*
Klaus Knorr and Sidney Verba, editors, *The International System: Theoretical Essays*
Sidney J. Ploss, *Conflict and Decision-Making in Soviet Russia*
Lucian W. Pye, *Guerrilla Communism in Malaya*

GPSR Authorized Representative: Easy Access System Europe - Mustamäe tee
50, 10621 Tallinn, Estonia, gpsr.requests@easproject.com

www.ingramcontent.com/pod-product-compliance
Lightning Source LLC
Chambersburg PA
CBHW050422280326
41932CB00013BA/1957